EARLY FINNISH ART

EARLY FINNISH ART

FROM PREHISTORY TO THE MIDDLE AGES

Photographs by István Rácz

With an Introduction by C. F. Meinander and Notes on the Illustrations by Pirkko-Liisa Lehtosalo

Translated from Finnish by Diana Tullberg

FREDERICK A. PRAEGER, *Publishers*

New York • Washington • London

FREDERICK A. PRAEGER, *Publishers*

111 Fourth Avenue, New York, N.Y. 10003, U.S.A.

77–79 Charlotte Street, London W.1, England

Published in the United States of America in 1967 by

Frederick A. Praeger, Inc., Publishers

This volume was originally published in 1961 in Finnish by

The Otava Publishing Company, Helsinki, Finland, under the title of

KIVIKIRVES JA HOPEARISTI:

Suomen Esihistorian Taideaarteita

Library of Congress Catalog Card Number: 67-15669

Printed in Finland

CONTENTS

A REVIEW OF FINNISH PREHISTORY

About 10,000 or 15,000 years ago the great continental ice sheet was beginning to melt and move away to the northwest. As the grip of the ice loosened, the land of Finland began gradually to emerge from the sea. Scattered rocks and tiny islands merged into bigger islands, then into archipelagoes, and thus, bit by bit, the Finland we know from the modern map was formed. The land is still slowly rising, but even as long ago as the Stone Age the coastline was roughly the same shape as it is now.

It took time before plants and trees reached Finland and began to take root. The birch was the first forest tree to arrive, soon followed by the pine, and finally by the fir, which did not begin to be common in western Finland until some 3,000 years ago.

The first of the big game animals to reach here was the reindeer. They felt at home on the treeless tundra and probably wandered here with the retreat of the continental ice, as the frozen earth yielded up new grazing land and space where they could follow their roaming instinct. Then, with the forests, followed the elk and bear and most of the small wild animals that still live in Finland's forests.

The first living things suitable for food, however, were fish and wild fowl. As the ice melted, it dammed up and formed a large fresh-water inland lake out of the waters of the Baltic. This explains the phenomenon of the fresh-water fish that are to be found in rivers that flow into the Baltic, which now has salty water. The food supply influenced the arrival of man in Finland, too, for wherever there was fish, people came. Big game and wild fowl were, of course, coveted, but Stone Age man's everyday food was fish.

The first people arrived in small groups and settled on the coast or made their way inland along the rivers to the shores of the fish-rich lakes. They had no regular dwelling places and wandered from one spot to the next, looking for the best fishing grounds and discovering where the reindeer went on their autumn and winter travels. Year after year they returned to the best fishing places, and at these points rich deposit strata gradually built up. Archaeologically, these Stone Age habitations yield great treasures. From broken and mislaid stone tools, clay pots, and ornaments, remains of dwellings and, best of all, from graves, the archaeologist can piece together a jigsaw, which, as it takes shape, spreads before us the cultural history of the Stone Age.

This book will perhaps give too grand and one-sided a picture of the Finnish Stone Age. From finds in neighboring countries we know that the fishermen and hunters of the Stone Age made a very large proportion of their implements from bone or horn, but these are materials that the topsoil in the sandy regions where Stone Age man lived very rarely preserved. In Finland, we have not found a single stone tool with the handle intact. We know what the stone blades of implements looked like, but know little of how they were used. We know what kind of clay vessels there were and are roughly aware of how they were decorated at various times in the Stone Age, but we know nothing of their purpose. We do not know anything about the people's language, almost nothing about their society, and very little about their beliefs.

The first people came immediately after the retreat of the continental ice sheet, attracted by the thousand-strong herds of reindeer ranging the treeless tundra. There are no archaeological finds from the Finland of that period, but there are some from farther north. The ancient banks of the Arctic Ocean, which can geologically be dated at around 8000 B.C., have yielded primitive tools in stone, reminders of man who lived at a time when Finland was still held fast in the grip of the ice. These finds represent what is called Komsa culture, the name coming from the place where they were found in Norwegian Lapland. The implements and weapons are made out of the types of stone and quartz native to the region, and some are so primitive in shape that it has been seriously considered that they might date back to a period previous to the last Ice Age.

The oldest Stone Age finds in southern Finland are what is called Askola culture (the finds were mainly made in the parish of Askola in eastern Uusimaa). They dated back to the seventh or possibly even eighth millennium B.C. The objects found are almost entirely in quartz. It is not until the end of this period that the first stone axes appear.

The finds from the sixth, fifth, and fourth millennia B.C. are called Suomusjärvi culture, after the parish in southwest Finland where a particularly large number of remains have been found. Most of our primitive stone axes, leaf-shaped slate weapon-heads, and a lot of the perforated clubs belong to this period. The small objects, arrowheads, scrapers, knives, and chisels are made of quartz. Suomusjärvi culture, we have concluded, lasted a long time — about 3,000 years. Some discernible advancement seems to have been made, but our knowledge of the period is so far very vague, not least because there are no ceramics among the finds. The period is also called Pre-Ceramic.

The oldest of our ceramic finds dates from around 3000 B.C. It should be mentioned immediately that this dating is rather summary and liable to correction by some 500 years in either direction. This new discovery, pottery, is not likely to have meant as much to Stone Age man as it does to the modern researcher, who can use it to classify finds more exactly both chronologically and geographically. Stone Age clay vessels are almost always heavily decorated and the style changes rapidly from one century to the next.

Throughout the third millennium B.C. and the beginning of the second, Finland was in the sphere of comb ceramics culture, as was the whole of the coniferous and mixed forest region of eastern Europe from the Wisla to the Urals and from the upper reaches of the Dnepr and Don to the North Arctic Ocean. The clay vessels from this culture were large egg-shaped pots, sometimes even a couple of feet high, and for decoration various kinds of stamps and circles or irregularly shaped squarish hollows, arranged in horizontal rows, were used. The most typical kind of decoration is the mark of a tooth-edged stamp, whence the name »comb ceramics.» The decoration is not the same everywhere. Only in Karelia and occasionally in Estonia is it exactly the same as in Finland.

Comb ceramics reaches its technical and artistic peak at the end of the third millennium B.C., after which we can, in a certain sense, speak of its decline. After 1600 B.C. it no longer appears at all. Large quantities of fragments of clay vessels have been found in settlements dating back to the comb ceramics period, but it has rarely proved possible to glue these pieces into complete vessels. There are seven large complete comb ceramics vessels in Finland and a few small cups and drinking bowls (plates 8—12).

The decoration of comb ceramics clay vessels is almost entirely ornamental and it is rare to find stamps of birds or people. The same geometrical decoration can sometimes be found on stone objects, too, especially on clubs and perforated weapons made of soapstone. Even so, we have not been able to date a single one of them for sure, and most of them may well belong to the Pre-Ceramics period.

The stone tools of the comb ceramics era are more varied in shape than those of the Pre-Ceramics period. It can even be called a time of awakening and experimentation. One of the most typical stone objects of the period is a small chisel (plate 20). It turns up in Karelia and Estonia as well as in Finland. During the comb ceramics period Finland also produced some completely individual sharp-edged perforated weapons not found anywhere else in the territory where comb ceramics culture was prevalent. This phenomenon may point to an influence from the west, as people there were already using perforated war axes made of stone at that time. The shape of the stone objects varies from place to place, owing largely to the different ways used to split the various types of stone. In western Finland we mainly find that only eruptive types of stone were used, and weapons struck out of these were necessarily a different shape from those made, for example, out of the fine Aunus green slate of Karelia.

Even in the comb ceramics period western and northern Finland were obviously to some extent in touch with the Scandinavian peninsula; but even so, the most important contacts were with the east. It appears, for example, that ceramics have been found in a number of settlements spreading from a center around the Upper Volga and its tributary the Oka. These clay vessels are decorated merely with rounded hollows, and the comb motif is not used at all. Similar ceramics have been found not only in the Ladoga region of Karelia and in East Karelia, but even as far west as the parish of Kymi in Uusimaa province. An interesting proof of associations between Finland and eastern Europe is, too, that objects made out of cembra pine have been found here. As far as we know, in the Stone Age, this variety did not grow farther west than the Zapadnaya Dvina River.

The most important import from eastern Europe was, of course, flint. Throughout the Stone Age flint was the chief, and in many places in Europe the only, raw material for stone vessels and implements. Almost no flint occurs naturally in Finland, and the people of the Stone Age therefore had to resort to a substitute, quartz, which was common and plentiful but much more difficult to work. But during the comb ceramics period, so much flint made its way here from the east that we can with reason talk of systematic trading. It was certainly brought from the Valdai area, but probably from elsewhere in northwest Russia too. So much of the same type of flint as in Finland has been found in settlements around the sources of the River Onega in the U.S.S.R. — both finished and half-finished work — that we can assume that the material occurred there naturally and was brought in some way to Finland. Only small objects were made out of this expensive imported material in Finland: arrowheads, scrapers and small knives. For axes they used native types of stone and for stabbing and cutting weapons often slate.

Amber was the gold of the Stone Age; 110 pieces of Stone Age amber jewelry have been found in Finland and only one of them has been proved to have come from the south of Scandinavia. This piece was found in Rovaniemi. All the others are the same type as the jewelry found on the southeast coast of the Baltic. These have been found in Stone Age settlements over a widespread area from the Gulf of Bothnia to the River Onega and right up to the upper sources of the Volga. In Schwarzort, in what used to be East Prussia, a number of pieces of Stone Age amber jewelry have been found while raising amber which are similar to those found here. We can thus assume that amber jewelry from that region was brought into Finland in the Stone Age.

The ornaments are rather simple in shape: mainly ground pieces of amber with a hole bored in them so that they could be worn on a thong as a necklace. A pendant like a human head has been found in Metsäpirtti in Karelia. Armlets are quite common, as are ax-shaped pendants, and a few singly and doubly perforated beads, buttons, and flat oblongs have been found. Amber was a valuable material, as valuable then as gold is now. In the Bronze Age and during the Roman period it was an expensive trading ware and was transported from the shores of the Baltic to the Mediterranean. Our own Stone Age finds show that this amber trading had long traditions. It would be interesting to know what Stone Age man gave his neighbors in return for this warm and glowing stone (plate 26).

Much of our amber has been found in Stone Age settlements, in graves, or in conditions pointing to burial. The most important place is Kolmhaara in Honkilahti, southwest Finland. Excavations there as recently as 1959 and 1960 revealed graves with contents which tripled our Stone Age amber jewelry collections. One grave alone produced fifty-six amber beads, another eleven.

Most pieces of amber jewelry date back to the »typical» comb ceramics period, when Finland and East Prussia, judging from their ceramics, belonged to the same culture. Imports continued throughout the Stone Age, however. But even when trading was at its height not everyone had had the chance or could afford to acquire some amber, and most had to be satisfied with simpler materials — stone or slate (plate 25). These substitutes are often similar in shape to the amber ornaments. Another popular ornament was a necklace made of animal teeth.

The appearance of imported wares in Finland indicates that Stone Age people went on long journeys, and luckily we also know something about their means of transport. We have found at the bottom of the lakes a number of simple boats made out of one piece of timber, and a couple of these have successfully been dated as Stone Age. A boat of this type and period, but so light that it should rightly be called a canoe, has been discovered in Helsinki. It was made from the trunk of a pine. It is, however, probable that there were also boats at that time with a keel and hoops, as it was not likely that men ventured out to sea in a round-bottomed boat or a light canoe. Perhaps skin-covered boats were used to ply the Gulf of Finland to Estonia or over the Kvarken and the Åland straits to Sweden. In strong currents, too, boats with a keel were almost certainly necessary. The elk head carved out of wood that was found in Rovaniemi probably decorated the prow of such a ship. It has been attributed to the Stone Age, with some reservations (plate 32).

Our oldest skis date from the Bronze Age, but since Stone Age skis have been found in northern Sweden and Norway, we can assume that they existed in Finland, too. A couple of dozen Stone Age sledge runners have been found here. There were, it seems, two types of sledge — one with two runners and a superstructure, the other with only one wide runner, the load being tied down onto it. Since early in the Stone Age the dog was a domestic beast, we can assume that these sledges were dog-drawn. The end of a sledge runner found in Heinola is decorated with an animal carving, probably a dog's head (plate 54).

Wooden objects from the Stone Age are rarely found — it is only in swamps and mire that they lie preserved for thousands of years. But very often such wooden objects are decorated with a carved animal head. As well as the carvings found in Rovaniemi and Heinola mentioned above, we have three spoons — from Laukaa, Pielisjärvi, and Kittilä — with a bear, duck, and elk carving on the handle (plates 34—35). These wooden spoons have been dated by pollen analysis, and it is possible that the last mentioned is rather later than Stone Age. The wooden carvings are at least as high quality as our famous stone carvings, and we can even safely assume that people first carved in wood, then in bone, and finally in stone.

Most stone carvings appear in the form of war axes and club heads. Twenty-two of these have been found in Finland. About ten were found in East Karelia, two farther east still, and two in Sweden. The models taken are the big game — elk and bear. The material is ground soapstone, in some cases gneiss, porphyry, and even quartz (plates 48—53).

The most famous of these is the Huittinen elk head (plates 48—49). It is the most naturalistic of all our Stone Age carvings and is said to represent a year-old calf that has just been killed. Also true to nature is the Säkkijärvi elk, the head of a war ax — it is said to be a cow elk which has just scented the hunter and is preparing to break into a run. The bears are more clumsily handled and on the other hand so stylized that it is difficult to recognize just what they are. The most beautiful are the Antrea, Heinävesi, and Paltamo carvings.

Why do we smile when we look at the only perforated ax in Finland and the world to be carved to represent a man? It produces the same reaction in everyone who sees it — a broad grin. Is it the delight of self-recognition? The museum visitor at last hits on man after peering at an endless row of stone axes (plate 47).

Four slate knives with carvings of animal heads make up a group of their own. They were all found in northern Finland, and the raw material is imported red slate from the north of Scandinavia. One of them reminds one of a waterfowl, another of a bear. The others are elk (plates 55—56). The animal head of the T-shaped implement found in Lapua (plate 30) and the little human figure from Rovaniemi, obviously worn as an amulet round the neck, are more random pieces.

Was it just the joy of portrayal that inspired Stone Age man when he carved the head of an animal on his wood or stone implements, or do these perhaps conceal religious ideas of a profundity that we can no longer know? The proposition has been put forward that these carvings are connected with the witchcraft of the hunt: a man supposedly gained control over a forest animal by making an image of it. Totemisms have also been detected in them: according to this theory Stone Age society had two clans, one with the elk as its totem, the other with the bear. We shall probably never know the truth.

But we do not find beauty only or even primarily in these animal carvings. Fine pictures are often the work of a skillful photographer. In other cases no picture could possibly do the objects justice. The Kiuruvesi gouge (plate 21) is one of the latter, a wonderful, faultless piece carved out of East Karelian slate, without a doubt our most beautiful Stone Age treasure. But do we not always acknowledge beauty whenever we see that the stonemason knows his craft, has chosen his material with an expert eye and has struck out an object as flawlessly functional as he planned? Beauty and ugliness are to some extent mere questions of taste, but to me a primitive and functional ax (plate 2) is more beautiful than a highly finished flint dagger (plate 59), which one suspects would snap with the first powerful blow.

We get only a very vague idea of Stone Age man's beliefs and cults from finds. Small human images made of fired clay, which are supposed to have been linked with some cult or other, have been found at comb ceramics settlements (plates 43—44). These »idols» are so stylized that it is often impossible to say whether they represent a man or a woman. They can to some extent be compared to the »Venus statuettes», miniature female images which appear in the centers of the early agricultural cultures of southeastern Europe and the Danube region. We can only guess what the idols were used for in these cults; in agricultural societies they were probably connected with the worship of ancestral spirits. If we study the idols we get some idea of what Stone Age people wore; in general, we know no more than that they knew how to twist fiber out of bast and nettles and that at the end of the third millennium B.C. they were using cloth. We can safely reject any romantic notions that Stone Age man had only animal skins and his own fine flowing locks to cover himself with.

The first people in Finland did not know anything about farming and had certainly not even heard of the strange customs of Syria and Palestine, where people had started living behind stone walls and expected to get nourishment from hay seeds put into the ground! Even when the first farmers of central Europe were burning clear their first patches of land around 4000 B.C. Finland was just going through the Pre-Ceramic period. It is probably true that the producers of comb ceramics knew of farming by hearsay, but they certainly felt scant respect for farmers who worked with dirty earth instead of ranging free through woods and over waterways.

Around the year 2000 B.C. a new people made their way into southwest Finland, the Hammer Ax tribe. They took their name from their fighting weapon, a boat-shaped hammer ax (plate 38). Articles belonging to Hammer Ax people have been found southwest of a line drawn between Kotka and Kokkola, in other words in the part of the country where the climate is mildest and where most of Finland's clay is found. The settlements are small and modest, and the graves — simple ground graves with no visible marks on the surface — usually occur singly. This indicates that the Hammer Ax people were wanderers and did not return every year to the same places, as the comb ceramics people did. They are thought to have been a nomad people who wandered from place to place searching for pasturage with their sheep and cattle — they possessed these animals, anyway.

As well as their boat-shaped war axes Hammer Ax people used well-made four-faced working axes (plate 40). Their clay vessels were rather small, often cups and pots with a twine decoration. The Hammer Ax people were probably familiar with corn cultivation: grindstones (plate 42) have been found near Hammer Ax settlements, and this may be evidence that they were Finland's first farmers.

The Hammer Ax people came here from Estonia, but their actual native region was certainly much farther away. At the same time as they were making their way to Finland closely related tribes were spreading over the whole of central Europe and Scandinavia. The boat-shaped war axes and twine-patterned pots typical of Finland's Hammer Ax tribe have been found as far west as Switzerland and Holland, as far south as Bohemia and the Ukraine, and as far east as the banks of the River Kama, a tributary of the Volga. Jutland, south and central Sweden, and southern Norway were also populated by the same people. There has been a lot of argument over the origins of the Hammer Ax people. Many archaeologists consider them Europe's first Indo-European people and believe they started out from an area north of the Black Sea. Others, on the other hand, think they came from the area between the Wisla and the Dnepr.

The oldest sure indications that metal was known in Finland date from the Hammer Ax culture. There are features in the boat-shaped war axes — for example, the fact that there is sometimes a »casting joint» along the back of the ax — which indicate that copper copies of the ax were cast in them. Finland's oldest copper article is a small plate found in Jettböle in Åland, which dates from the late Hammer Ax period.

Finds have been made in East Karelia which perhaps indicate that even as early as the typical comb ceramics period simple ornaments were being made out of copper. This is itself by no means impossible, since copper ornaments occur in central Europe as early as c. 2500 B.C. and in Denmark around 2300 B.C., but we must acquire some more conclusive finds before we can consider it certain that comb ceramics age man used copper. It is always possible that more recent objects have got mixed up in the strata at settlements.

The Finnish climate was obviously too inclement for the Hammer Ax tribe, since Hammer Ax culture disappears by 1000 B.C. at the latest. The people probably merged into the earlier population, as they certainly did not disappear altogether. The inhabitants of Finland learned from them how to herd cattle and, apparently, how to grow corn, and these two advances were among the most important occurrences in our history. We may, indeed, ask ourselves whether Finnish culture has ever since taken so decisive a step forward.

In another sense, too, Hammer Ax people played an important part in Finnish history. Finland (and Estonia) had previously come under an eastern European cultural influence. The Hammer Ax tribe opened a window to central Europe and Scandinavia, and ever since our dealings with the west have constantly widened in scope. At the end of the Stone Age, in what is called the Kiukainen culture era, a fairly large quantity of wares imported from Scandinavia appear close to the coast. Daggers and saws, for instance, were imported, made of southern Scandinavian flint. The interior and eastern Finland were, however, all this time in contact with nations to the east.

This geographical bipartition, which can be clearly distinguished as early as the late Stone Age, characterizes the following period of Finnish prehistory, the Bronze Age (1300—500 B.C.). In that period a form af culture which in many essential features is the same as that in other countries in Scandinavia prevailed in the southern and western coastal regions of Finland. The dead were buried in large stone barrows (»glacial boulder mounds») on top of rocky outcrops in the same way as they were on the coast of Sweden and the larger islands of the Baltic. The bronze articles found there are the same type as throughout the northern region centered on Denmark, and most of them were without any doubt imported. Here, too, people knew how to cast bronze implements, but the weapons came from as far afield as the Danube.

From finds at settlements, we get a slightly different picture of cultural conditions than that given by our rather sparse collection of bronze articles. We still find stone implements — of the same type as at the end of the Stone Age — and the clay vessels also demonstrate continuing traditions. But people no longer moved from place to place as they did in the Stone Age. They had apparently started a more settled farming life at the beginning of the Bronze Age at the latest, and the settlements of this period can already with every reason be called villages. At the same time, however, there were communities whose members made their living by deep-sea fishing and by catching seals.

The new invention, bronze, increasingly replaced stone as the material for axes, and the new method of farming changed modes of life. It was new immigrants from Sweden who introduced these new ideas, but they did not form their own separate communities and settled down side by side with the former inhabitants and soon integrated with them fully. No important population shifts have been noted in Finland's coastal regions in the Bronze Age.

In the interior, roughly the same kind of progress was being made. The only difference was that the most important influences came from the east, not from the west. Some bronze implements have been found in these areas, but they are similar in type to those found in northern Russia. The ceramics is the same as that found around the upper reaches of the Volga, around Lake Ladoga and Lake Onega. It is what is called textile ceramics, the name coming from the fact that there is an impression of fabric on the surface. Stone was still used to make axes, chisels, and scrapers — as was also the custom on the coast — and arrowheads were made of quartz or flint as before. There are, however, no Bronze Age barrows in the interior, or any finds which would point to a farming society.

Although many factors indicate that the inhabitants of the interior were descendants of the comb ceramics people, this cannot be proved beyond all doubt. Some archaeologists believe that the spread of textile ceramics and eastern European bronze objects westward to Finland and Estonia shows that a new people made their way here about 1000 B.C.

During the Bronze Age northern Finland formed a distinct cultural area side by side with the coastal regions and the lakeland uplands. The bronze articles are similar to those found in the north of Sweden and northern Norway, and in north and northwest Russia. A great number of soapstone molds have been found, which proves that bronze axes were cast in north Finland, too. The clay vessels are thin and a lot of asbestos has been mixed with the clay. It has been thought that this is the culture of the ancestors of today's Lapps, and from some finds it has been concluded that this culture goes on almost unchanged right through to the Iron Age, even up to the Middle Ages.

There is not much to say archaeologically about the period between 500 B.C. and the first century A.D. Finland's coastal culture, which soon moved on to other parts of Scandinavia, has left us no traces and the age of finds attributed to this period is in fact very uncertain.

About A.D. 100 a new period begins in Finland. All at once rich new sites for finds turn up in southwest Finland, which lead us to believe that a new people arrived here from overseas. It was the beginning of the Iron Age. What we know about the Iron Age is based primarily on burial finds. At that period the dead were fitted out with weapons and ornaments and buried in special cemeteries. Although the Iron Age finds are much more plentiful than those from Stone or Bronze Age, our knowledge of this era is nevertheless somewhat one-sided in that we know very little about Iron Age villages and settlements. This arises, for example, from the fact that modern Finnish villages have developed in exactly the same places as at the beginning of our calendar. Later buildings have thus wiped out all trace of older constructions.

Of the oldest cemeteries, we would give special mention to three. In the Karjaa parish on Kroggårdsmalm there is a burial ground dating from the first century A.D. Both the shape of the graves and the objects found there are exactly the same type as in Estonia at the same time, and the same type of cemetery has been found near the estuary of the River Kokemäki in Penttala, Nakkila. Most of the objects were the same Estonian type and seem to indicate that there had been settlements there before the first Estonian immigrants arrived. The third cemetery worthy of mention is in Kärsämäki, in Turku. These are cremation graves; the remains of the cremated body have been put into a clay pot or wooden box with the grave offerings, and buried or placed in a small hollow and protected with stone slabs. The articles are the same type as those found at the Wisla delta. It has therefore been assumed that this cemetery belonged to an immigrant community founded here by Goth merchants.

There are, too, some dozen cemeteries dating from the period called the early Roman Iron Age (A.D. 100—200), and these reveal that there have been three different ethnic elements here: the original settlers, emigrants from Estonia, and Germanic settlers. These three elements, over the centuries that followed, founded the Finnish nation.

One of the most interesting finds of the period is the Pernaja hoard. Near a large stone, which around A.D. 100 marked a water boundary, axes, spearheads, and sickles made of iron have been found. They are Estonian in type and probably belonged to an Estonian merchant traveler who had come to the coastal regions of Uusimaa to sell his wares. He had hidden some of them in a place where he could easily find them later, but for one reason or another never came back for them. That sickles appear on the scene here proves that somewhere in Uusimaa or farther north there were people who were interested in agricultural implements. Although we know almost nothing about these people, the Pernaja find indicates that before the great emigration from Estonia began, Finland was not just inhabited by wandering Lapps.

The fact that a new age dawned in Finland around A.D. 100 was the consequence of the situation in central Europe. Rome's legions still kept the peace around the Rhine and Danube, and there were lively trading contacts between Rome and free Germania. Rome's trade network did not reach as far as Finland, but its effects were felt here indirectly. From literary sources we know that the ancient Germans loved to dress themselves in expensive skins and that they bought these from the other side of the Baltic, thus also to some extent from Finland. Finland's Estonian and Gothic immigrants were trappers and fur merchants and had come here about A.D. 100 attracted by the chance of doing good business.

Some Roman ware has found its way to Finland too. We have, for instance, found two bronze wine scoops made in Italy and some Roman money.

All the earlier Roman Iron Age graves here are on the coast, in the area between Karjaa and Vöyri. During the later Roman Iron Age (A.D. 200—400) people settled more thickly on the Finnish coast and spread to the Kokemäki valley and to southwest Häme. The Gothic features of finds disappear and instead they now have a mainly Estonian stamp. The same period produces the first sure signs of the arrival of Swedish immigrants on our southwest coast and the coastal region of southern Ostrobothnia. The immigrants settled among the existing population and did not form any kind of enclosed group. During the great migration epoch (A.D. 400—800) settlements developed fast as far as the shores of Lake Päijänne, and in the Viking era (A.D. 800—1000), people were already living in Savo. The oldest of the Åland cemeteries to be dated with certainty is from the sixth century A.D., and from the ninth century onward the north shores of Lake Ladoga begin to be a heavily settled farming region.

Although fur trading introduced a new era and produced the first villages, Finnish society was still a peasant society. From the size of cemeteries we can conclude that people lived in villages of a handful of houses. Their fields were already well-established and they plowed with an iron share, but land clearance also played an important role. The people not only fished and hunted in their own neighborhood, but also went on long trips into the wilds, right up to the distant wastes of north Finland.

Iron was the usual general service metal and could be produced from Finland's own excellent lake ore, but the bronze and silver needed for jewelry had to be brought from visiting merchants from abroad. There were smiths and founders in the villages who knew how to make implements, weapons, and ornaments, but a lot of finished goods were also imported. In this way Finland kept up with central European fashions. And although there were purely national weapons and ornaments, Finland, generally speaking, followed development in the Germanic world right through the Iron Age. These, in turn, took their lead from the advanced weapon-making techniques and changes in jewelry fashion of the Mediterranean countries. Finland began to form part of the great cultural body of Europe.

Each peasant was also a warrior, and his full armor consisted of a sword, shield, and one or two spearheads. The fashion in weapons changed as time went on and was, of course, also dependent on the warrior's wealth. The poorer peasant had to be content with one spearhead or ax and only the rich could afford the luxury swords shown in plates 103 and 104. Shields were round and made of wood, though they had an iron boss in the middle against which the warrior fended off sword blows. He took his weapons with him to the grave, but often they were twisted out of shape just to make sure that the dead man's spirit would not rise from the grave and attack the living.

Women's jewelry was mostly made out of bronze. Silver is rare, and of the armlets found only about a dozen are in gold. The latter metal is rather more common in the form of gilding. At the beginning ot the Iron Age east Baltic jewelry was copied rather slavishly, but in the fifth century a slight effort at independence can be noted. In the sixth century increasing amounts of purely Scandinavian jewelry forms appear, and from the seventh century on these hold the ascendancy over east Baltic styles, although the latter crop up to some degree

16

right through the prehistoric period. The ornaments were bracelets and necklaces, strands of glass beads and various pendants on the one hand, and on the other brooches and waist-buckles, which played an important part in the complete outfit. Shoulder-buckles were usually worn in pairs and held the dress up at the shoulders, whereas a single buckle was used to fasten together the fronts of the blouse. A woman's outfit also, at the end of the Iron Age at least, included an apron, profusely decorated with small bronze spirals, and a large shawl or cape. The material used was mainly home-woven wool or linen, but foreign cloth was also used.

Something must also be said about the ornamentation of the articles found. During the Roman Iron Age, ornament is scanty: almost entirely just groups of lines or various kinds of stamps. The east Baltic fashion in jewelry does not usually involve ornamentation and emphasizes interesting shapes. The everyday curved buckles, for example, rely on interesting protuberances. The Germanic style of decoration, which from the sixth century on is the greatest influence on Finland, is itself influenced by the art of late antiquity in the Mediterranean countries. The oldest animal ornamentation is relatively naturalistic, but in the hands of Germanic and Scandinavian smiths the animal body is broken down into its components and these are given geometrical shapes. This is the main sixth-century style. In the seventh and eighth centuries, the animal heads, bodies, tails, and limbs are twisted and plaited together and set against complex abstract twinings (plate 96). The ninth and tenth centuries also have their own animal styles. It is not until the twelfth century that animal ornamentation is fully abandoned and coils of acanthus leaves and floral motifs, originating in romantic models common to all of European art, take its place.

Coins have been found here and there, but we can be sure that money was not used in the same sense as nowadays. The oldest money finds in Finland are copper, struck with images of the Roman emperors. Some Roman gold coin has been found in graves of the fifth and sixth centuries, all from the flourishing regions of southern Ostrobothnia, which traded with Hälsingland, Tröndelag, and Gotland. It is not until the Viking period that money becomes more common. In the ninth and tenth centuries a considerable amount of the trading done between western Europe and the Near East was carried out via the Baltic, and this meant that large quantities of Arabian silver coin and jewelry entered the north. The Finnish silver collections from this period are, it is true, modest compared with the Swedish finds, but they nonetheless prove that Finland took her share of this copious flow of silver. The eleventh century is mainly a period for German and English silver coin.

At the end of the Iron Age the value of silver dropped, as rich silver mines were found in the eastern parts of the Arab empire. Our biggest silver treasures from this period have been found in Lapland. The most valuable of the fur-bearing animals, sable and beaver, had probably already disappeared from southern Finland, and buyers had to make their way far into the north if they wanted to acquire these coveted skins. The pelts were paid for in silver, possibly in necklaces and bracelets made of melted-down coin. Some of the jewelry found in Lapland had obviously been made specially for the Lapps, such as the large silver pendant in plate 140. The thick necklaces made of twisted strands of silver are of a type that turns up throughout northern and eastern Europe. The horseshoe-shaped buckles decorated with acanthus leaves found in Lapland have, on the other hand, otherwise been found only in Karelia around Lake Ladoga. It has therefore been assumed that they were made in Karelia and that the entire trade with Lapland was carried out by Karelians. It is possible, however, that all this silver jewelry came from the workshops of Novgorod, and that the merchants of this town — at that time the most important trading center in northern Europe — had acquired the sole rights to the fur trade. The Karelians would then have acted only as buyers for them, much in the way the Canadian fur dealers do today.

We know very little about the beliefs of pagan Finns, and the little knowledge we have has been culled from old poetry rather than from finds. There are a few later indications of the deities worshiped by the Finns and Karelians, but when we study these gods more closely, we see that most of them merely cloak the identity of some medieval saint. We can say for sure only that people believed in some mighty spirit or ruler of the heavens, and in countless sprites of land and water. The worship of ancestral spirits played an important role in cult rites, and communities had their own soothsayers, who acted as intermediaries between man and the supernatural. Shamanist features have also been detected in ancient Finnish faiths.

The foundation stone of society was the family and the clan, the head of which had absolute authority. No larger community than clan and village have been shown to exist, but there may have been unions of families and villages. The province name »Satakunta» (»The Hundreds») would seem to indicate the same kind of larger unified association as the »hundars» of central Sweden, which eventually formed the kingdom of Svea. It has also been thought that the construction of so large a defense work as Rapola Castle on Sääksmäki hill in southern Häme must certainly have required the backing of a bigger community than a mere village. The ancient sagas of Iceland tell that the Norsemen made an agreement with the king of the Finns on a campaign to be made against the Karelians. Should there be any basis of truth in these tales, the »king» involved was presumably some leader of a Finnish expedition to northern Finland. It is hardly likely that there were any actual kings here at that date.

The law was »right through custom» and was dispensed by the elders of the community. It is not likely that there was any actual judge's post, and, of course, there was no written law. The prehistoric period ends in southwest Finland around the year A.D. 1150 and 100 years later in Karelia. The boundary between prehistoric and historic seems more rigid than it is, since at a certain stage the archaeologists defer to the historians, and these two disciplines tackle their problems in different ways.

Christianity rejects the pagan custom of putting articles in graves, and thus the one source from which archaeologists draw most of their facts when studying the cultural history of the Iron Age dries up. To begin with, literary sources, i.e., historical sources proper, are very rare and say little, and we can without exaggeration claim that we know more about prehistoric Finland than we do about the thirteenth and fourteenth centuries. But the boundary between prehistory and history is no mere formality. It involves a fundamental revolution in society. Previously there had been no governmental power and no church. Afterward, the country was linked to the Kingdom of Sweden and the Roman Catholic Church. The small surplus that farming and hunting expeditions into the wilds had brought, and which had earlier been used for modest luxuries, now went to state and church taxes. In return, the state promised security and the the church eternal life. There is no reason to think that people were on the whole dissatisfied with the exchange.

New, too, were the towns, which at one blow revolutionized trading and attracted artisans. The peasants had to give up their journeys to distant lands, and the village smiths had to rest content with forging plowshares and horseshoes. The most talented and enterprising tried to get jobs in the towns or in the service of church or state. The beginning of history thus meant an impoverishment of peasant society in many respects.

According to tradition, southwest Finland was converted to Christianity in A.D. 1155, Häme in 1248, and Karelia in 1293.

C. F. MEINANDER

I

2

3

6

7

9

10

12

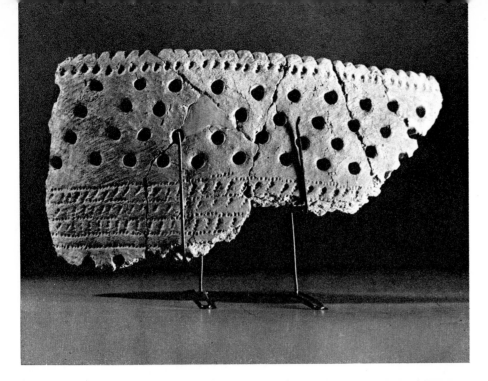

13

14

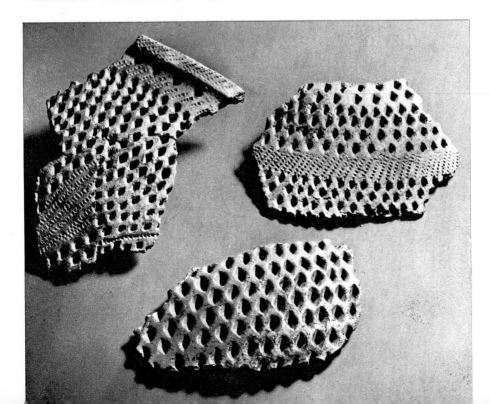

15

54676

17

19

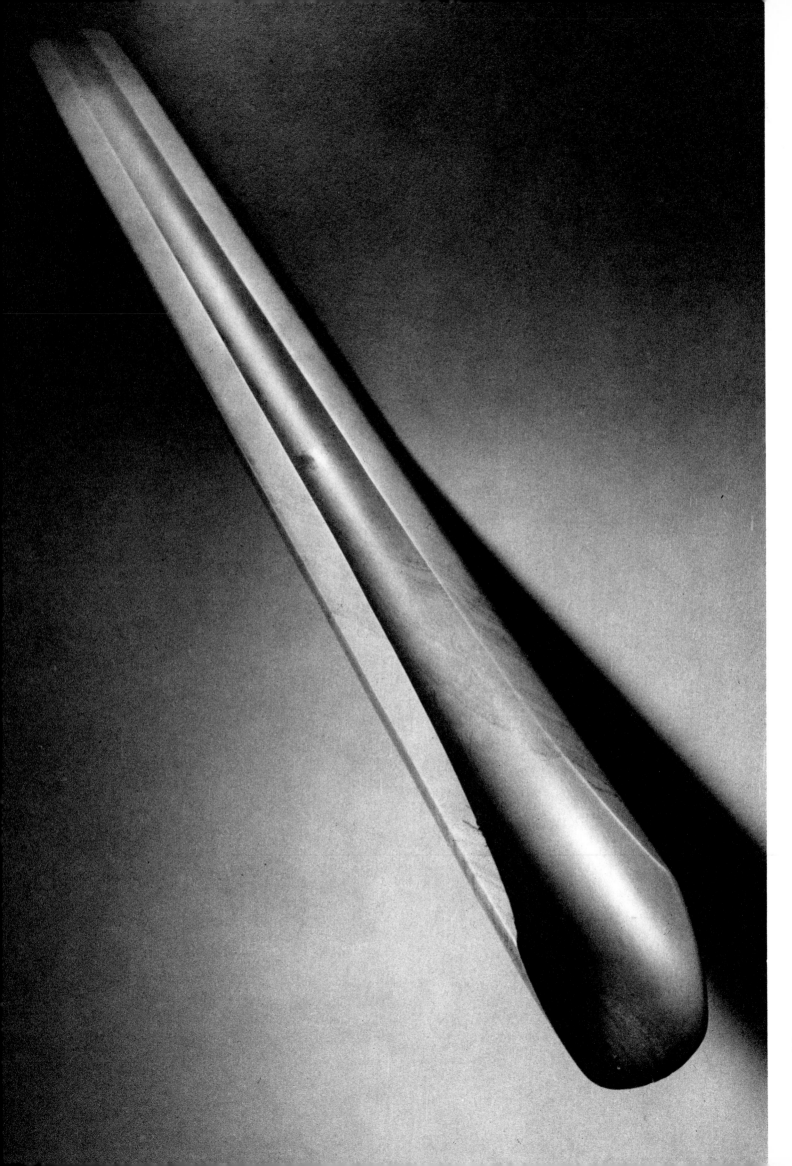

Rácz

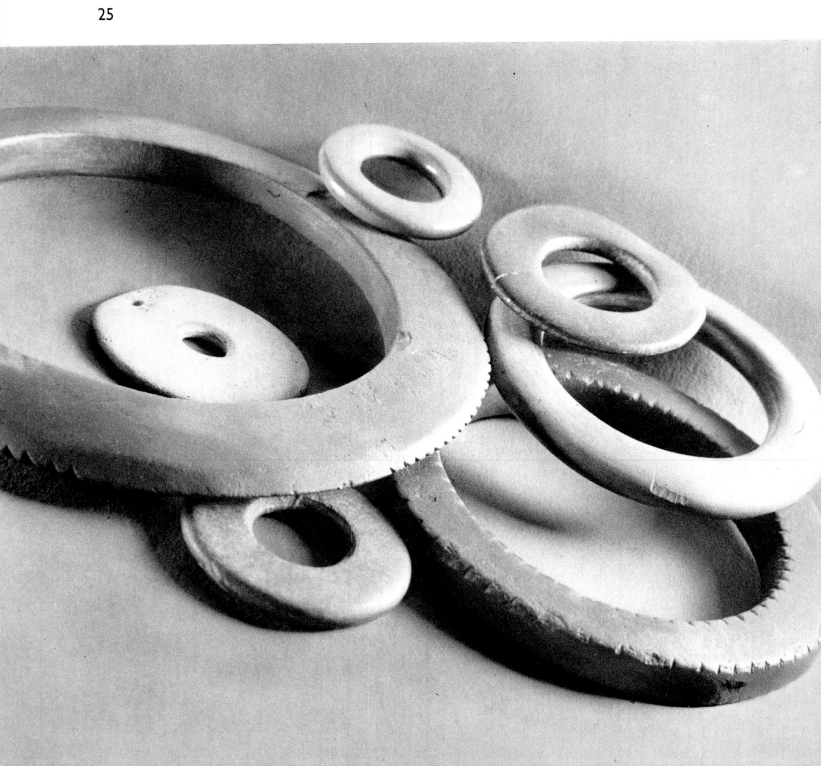

26

27

28

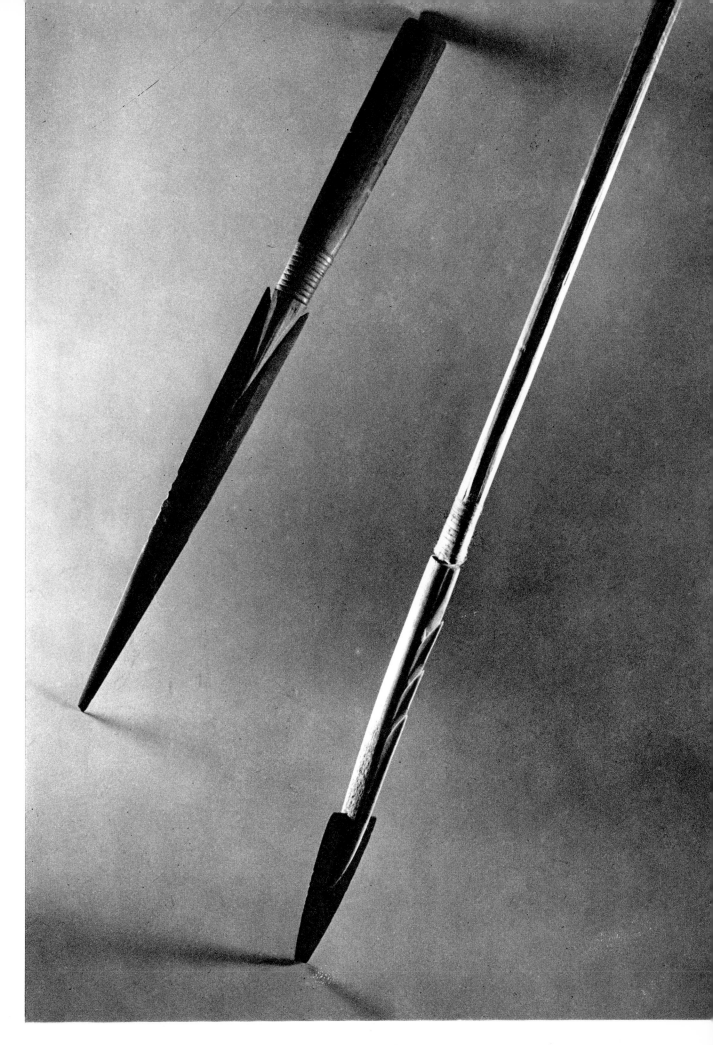

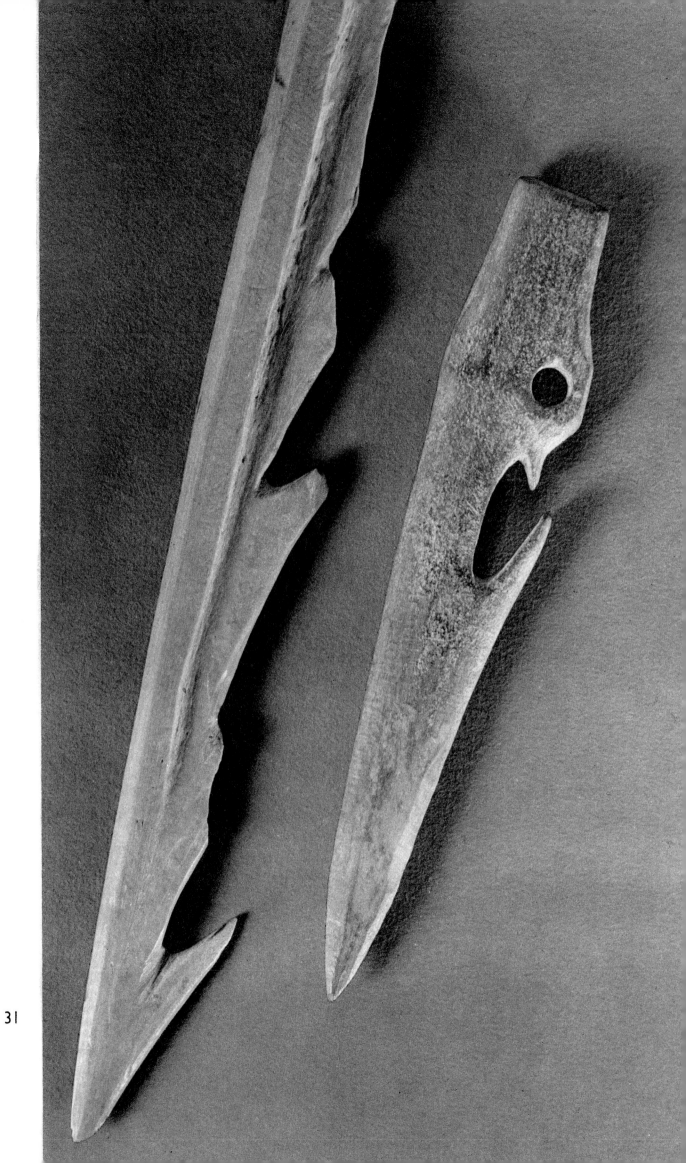

31

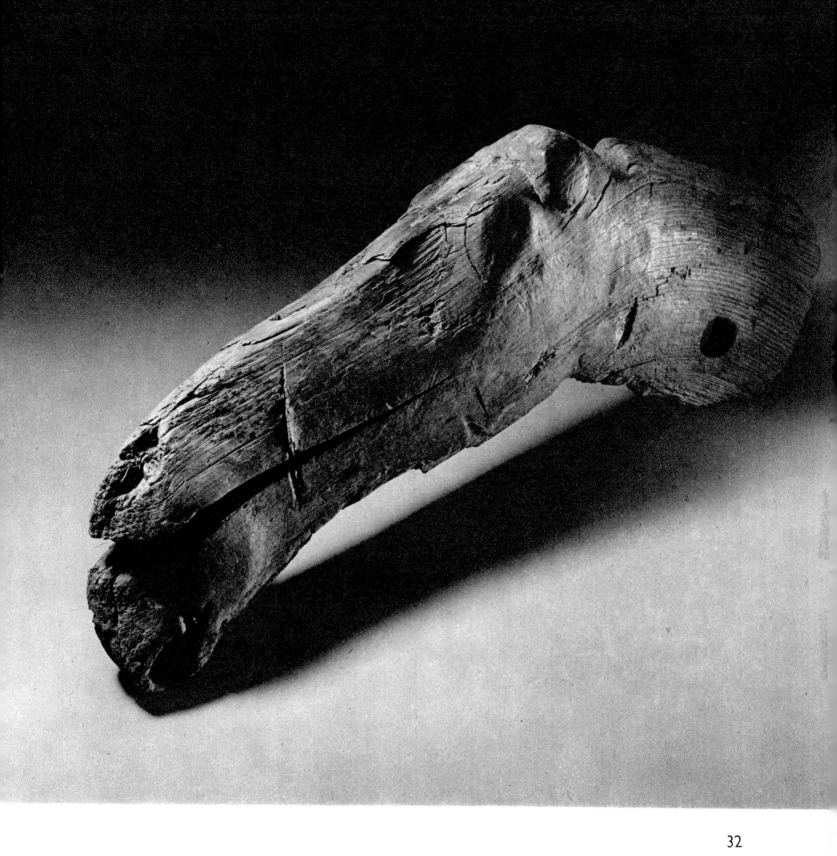

34

36

39

40

41

42

43

45

46

47

48

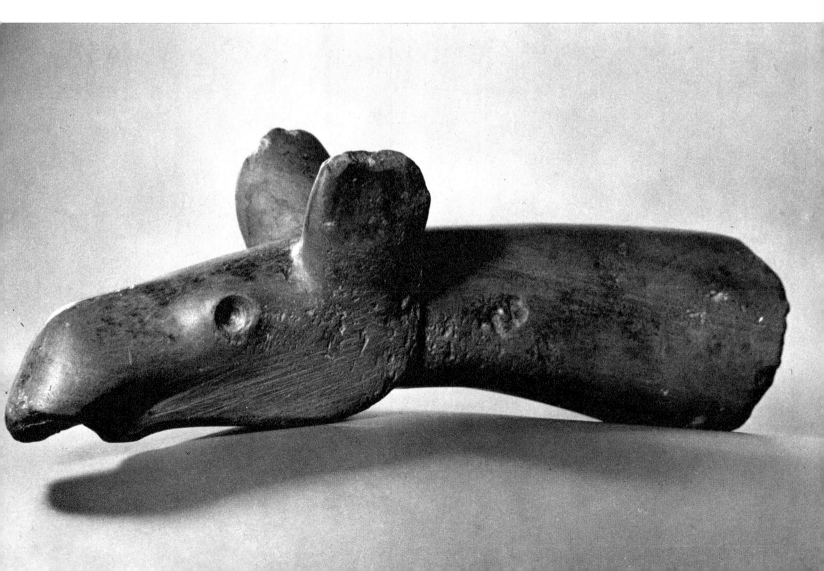

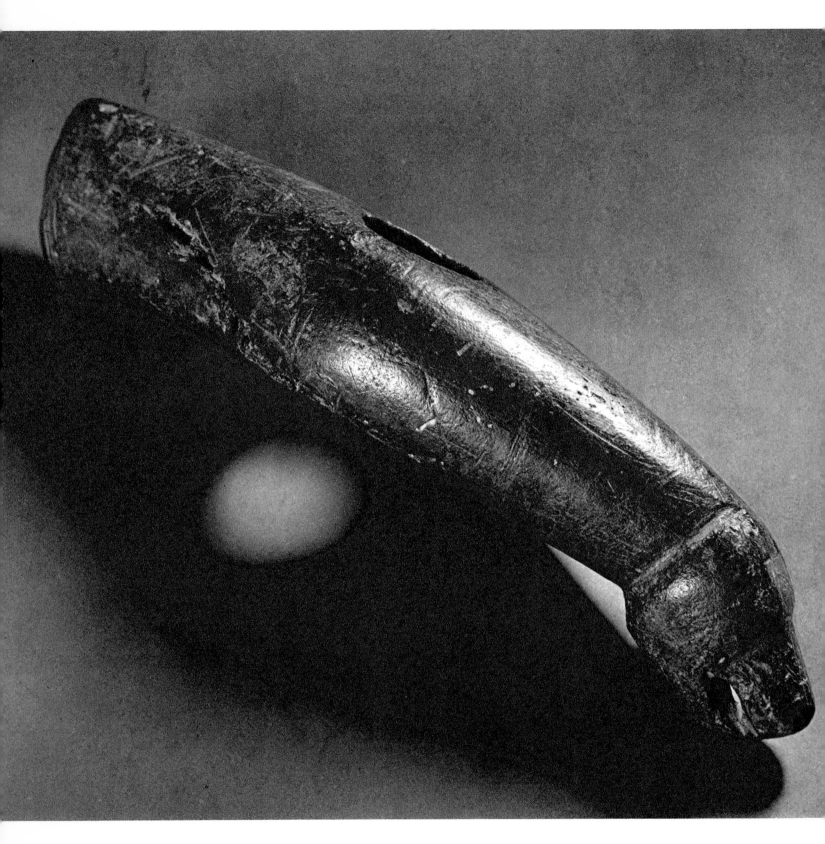

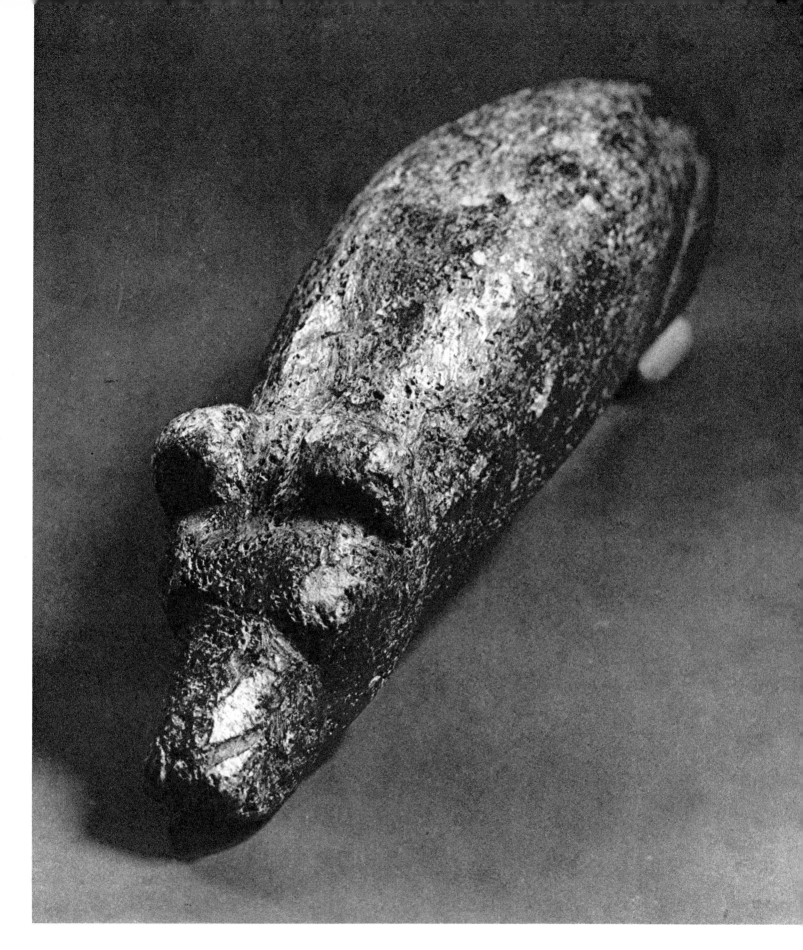

57

60

61

62

65

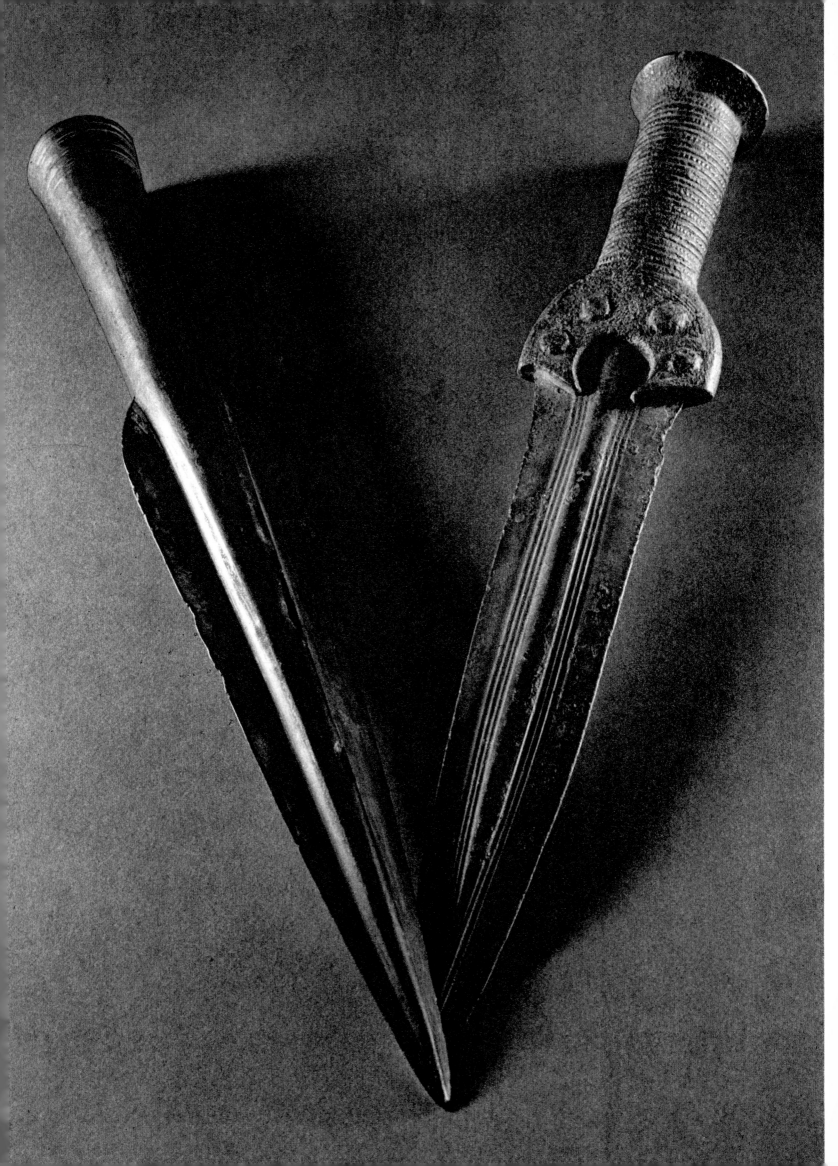

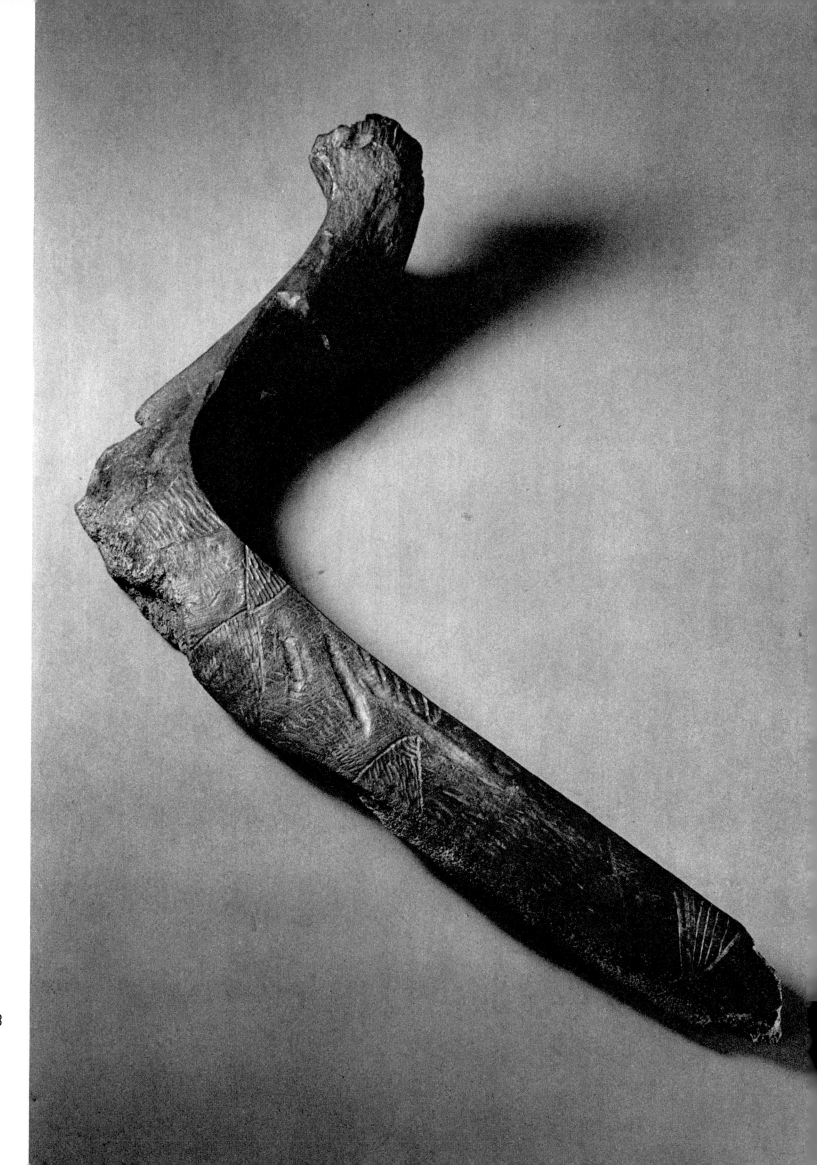

71

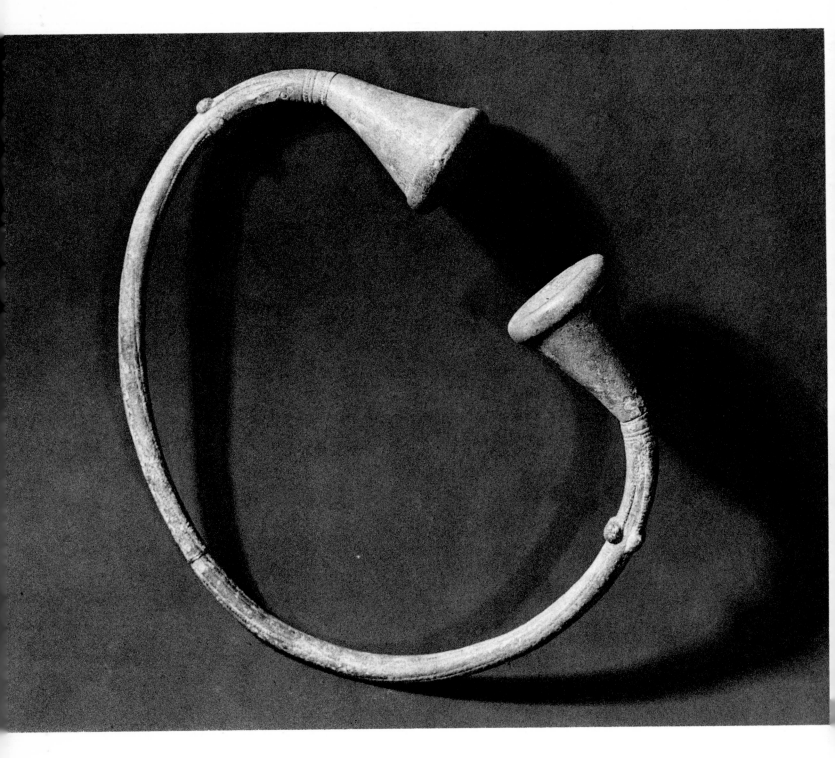

74

75

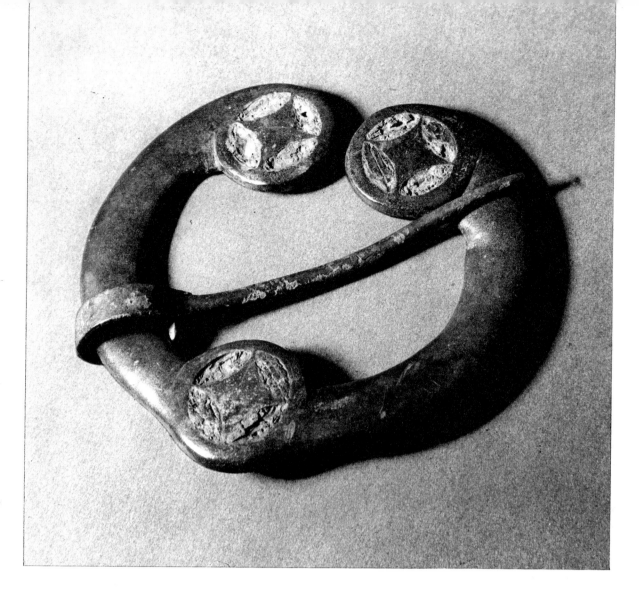

77

78

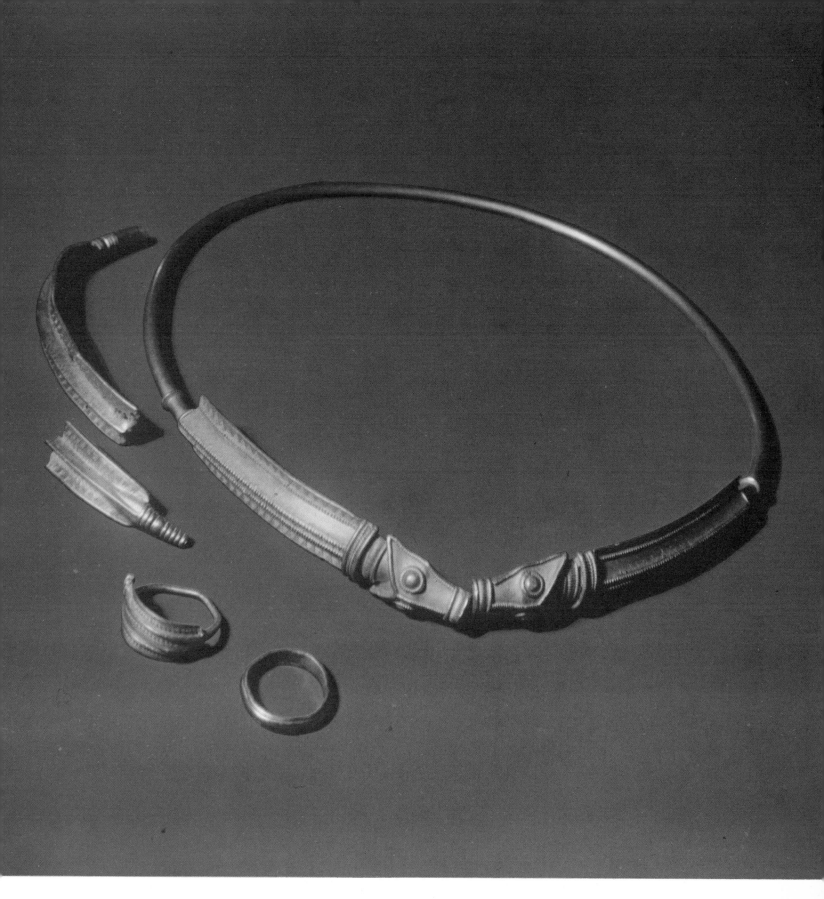

84

88

89

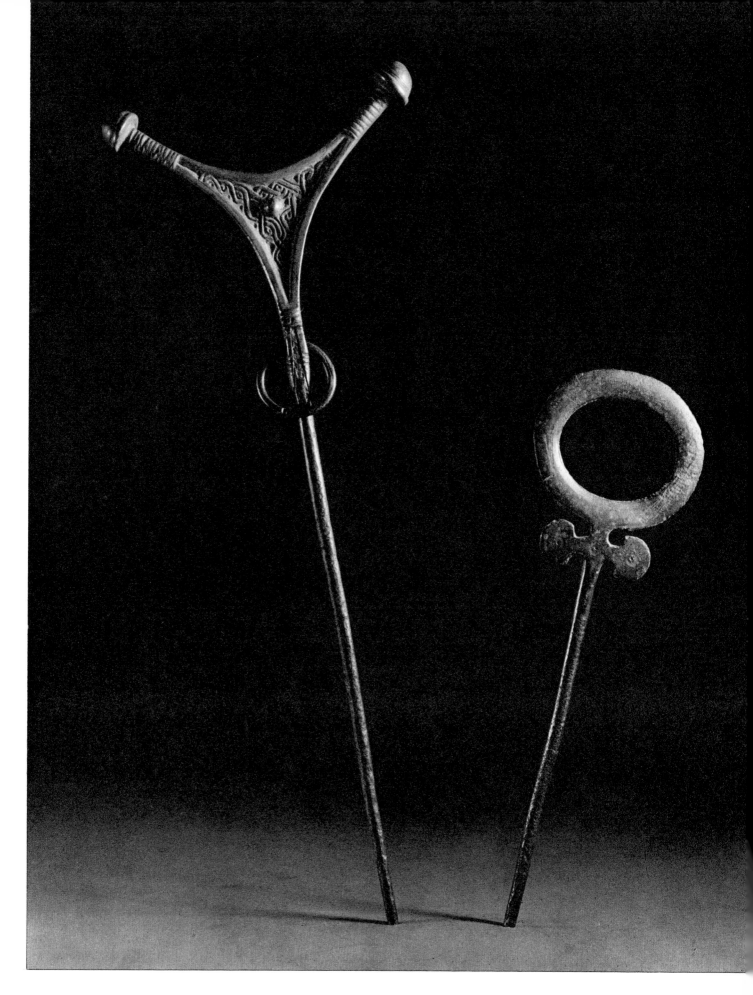

93

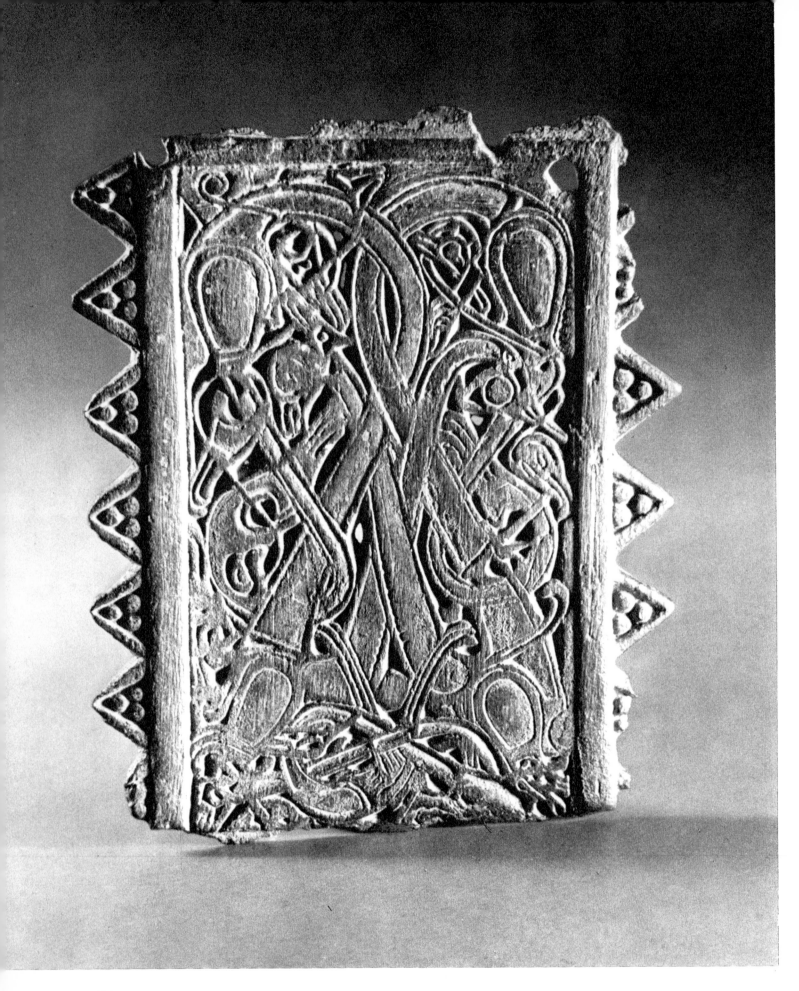

98

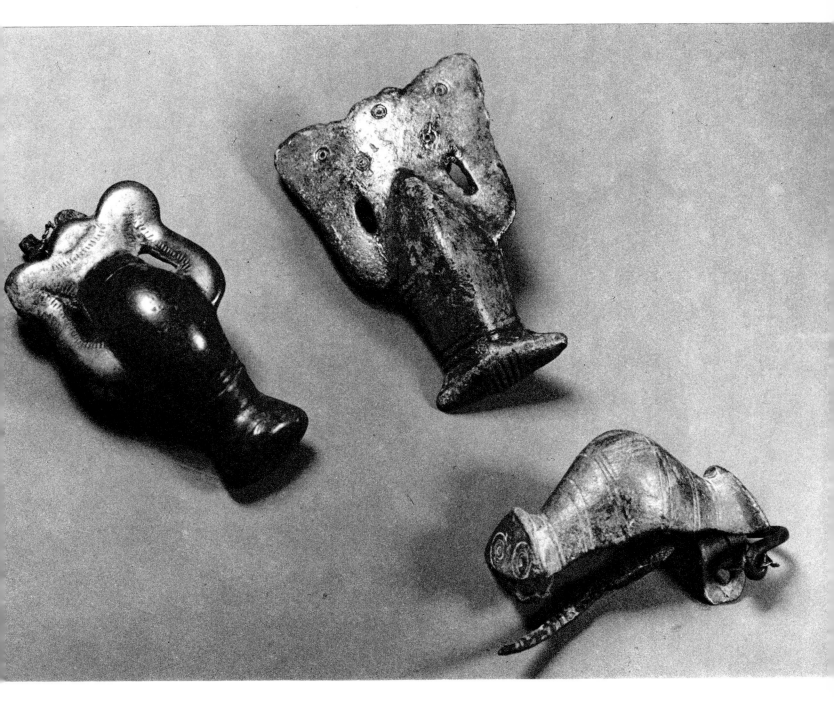

100

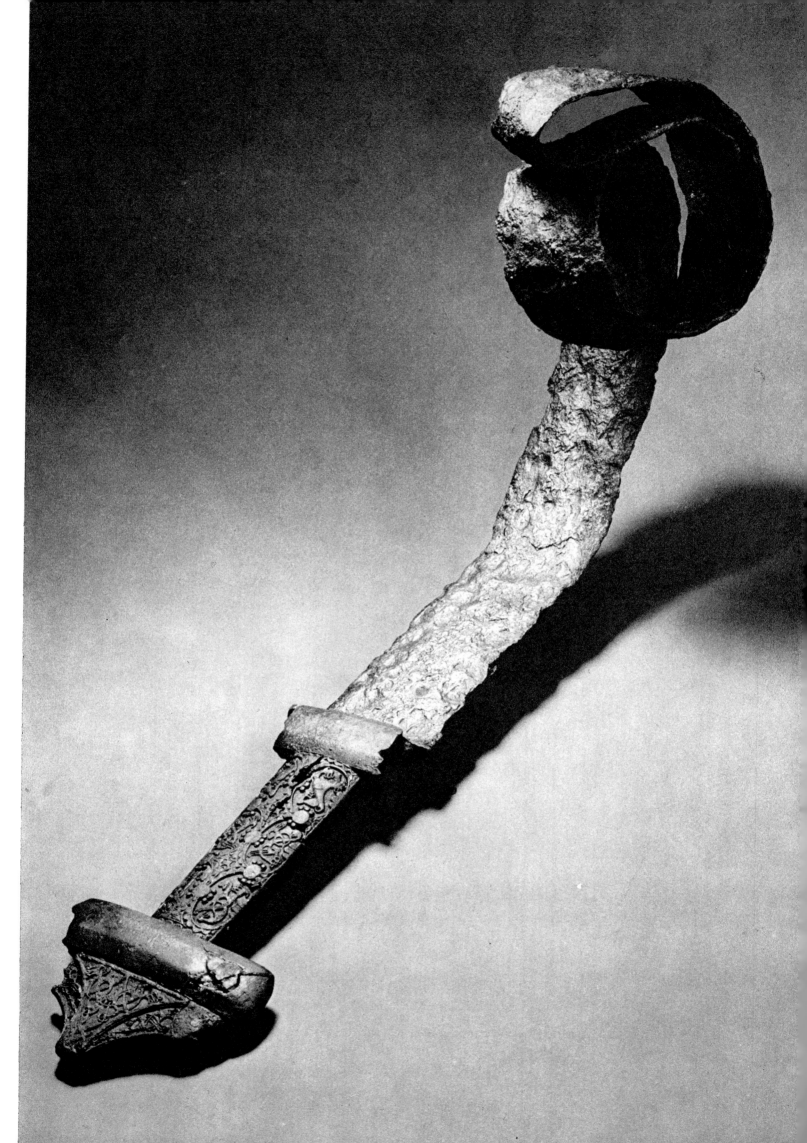

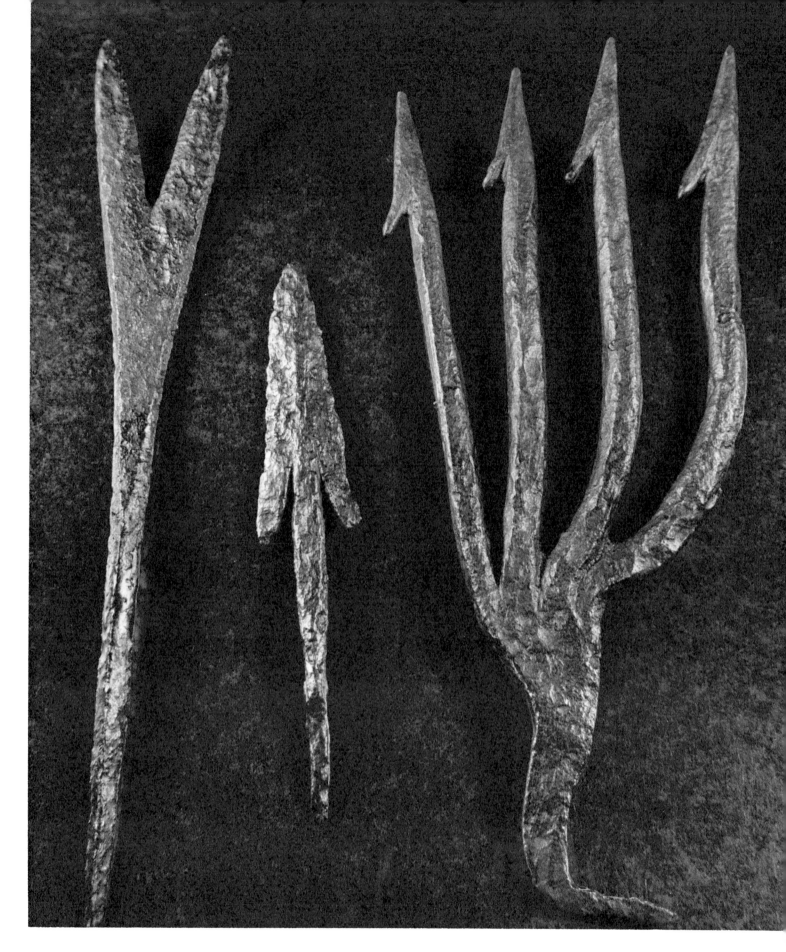

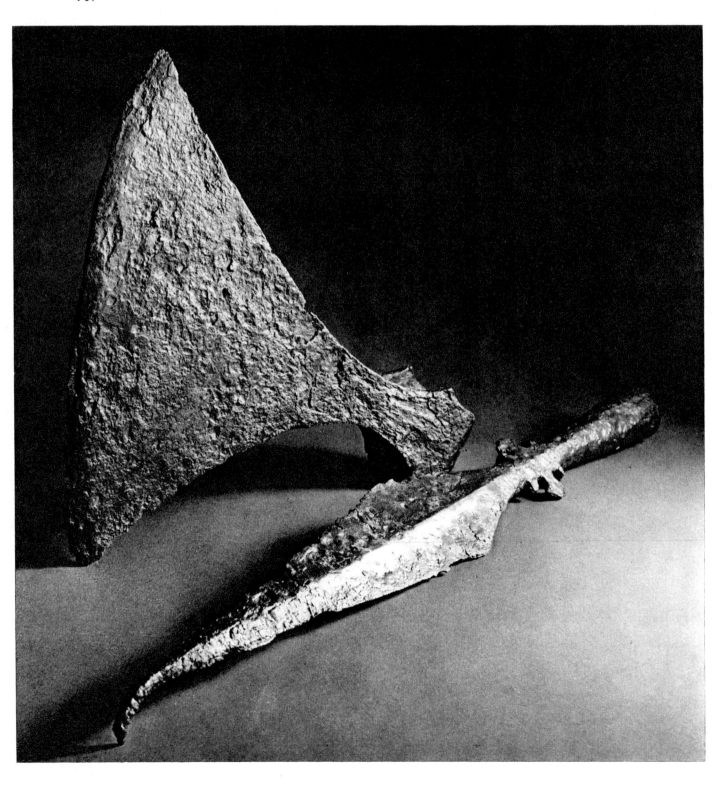

115

117

118

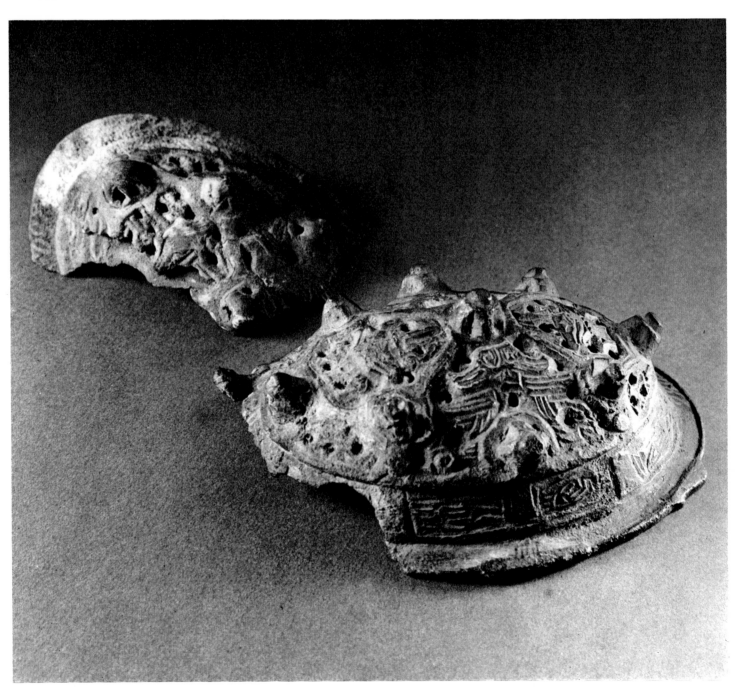

121

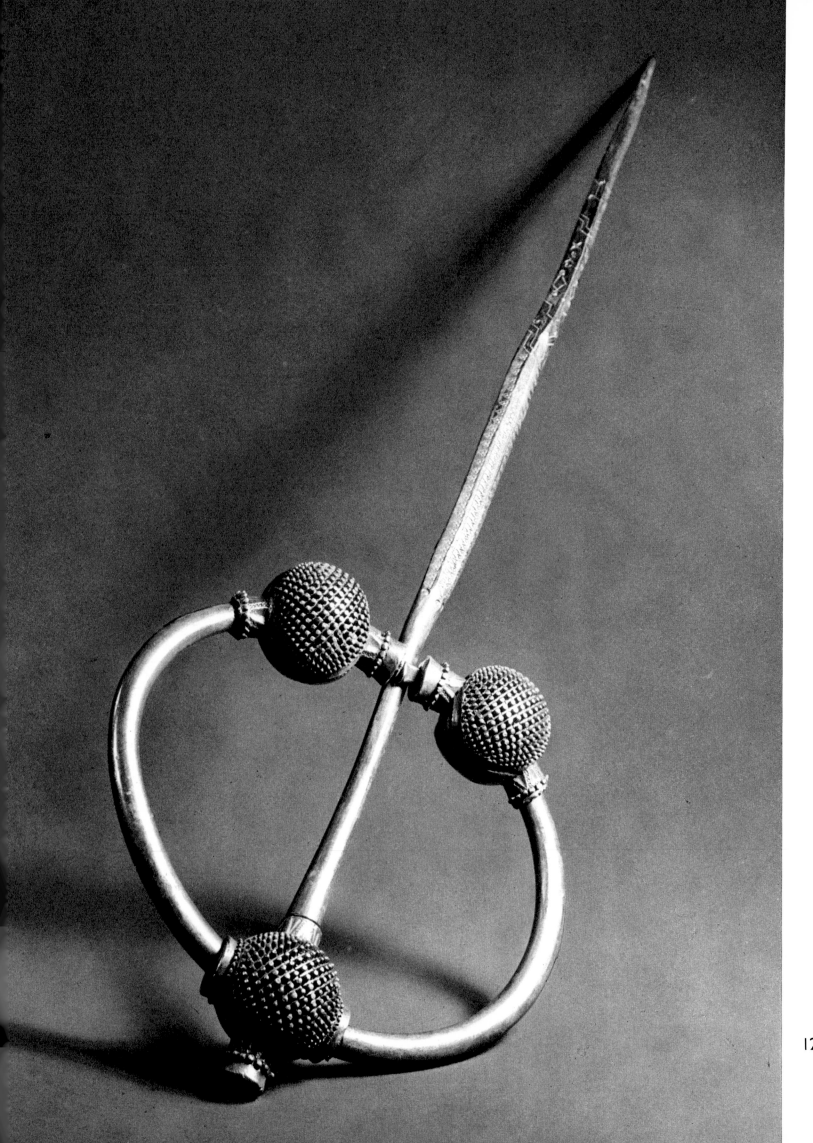

126

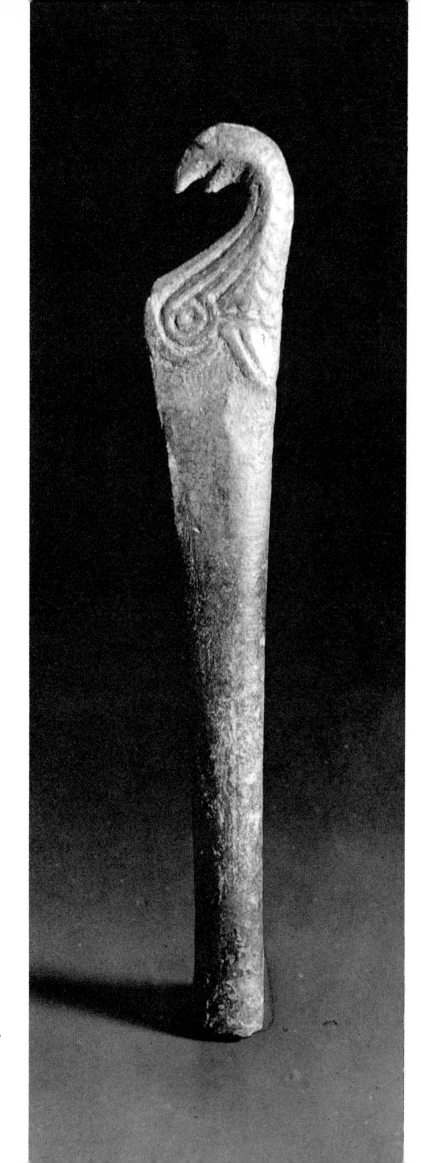

127

128

129

134

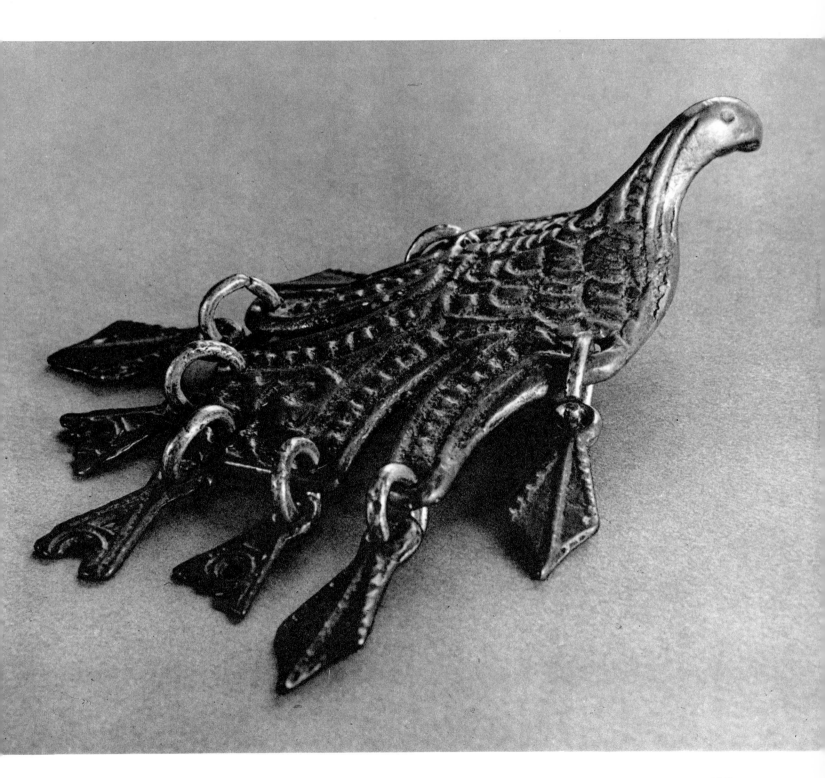

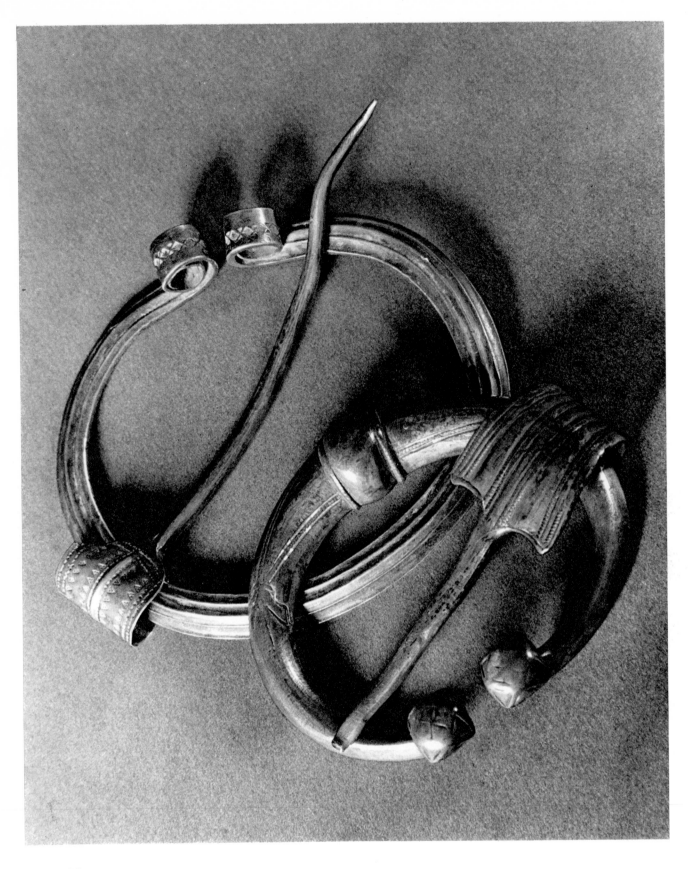

138

139

140

142

144

145

148

154

155

PLATES

All dimensions are given in inches, followed by millimeters in parentheses.

1

»Parrot's beak-shaped groove maker.» This quartz piece was found in Kopinkallio, Nakkila, in Askola, where there was a quartz quarry during the Askola culture period. At a guess, Askola culture goes back some 9,000 years and such groove makers were a typical article. They were used for drawing on bone, wood, or horn. National Museum 12661:1633.
1 $^3/_4$ × 1 $^1/_{16}$ × $^3/_8$ (44 × 26 × 9 mm.)

2

Unfinished stone ax from Koivisto in Sammatti, where there was a settlement in the Suomusjärvi culture period. (5500 — 3000 B.C.).
NM 6936:5. 5 $^3/_8$ × 2 $^{15}/_{16}$ × 1 $^5/_{16}$ (135 × 74 × 33 mm.)

3

Stone axes from the Suomusjärvi culture period. The two axes at the top are unfinished. The rest are finished with the grinding work concentrated on the blade. The one in the middle is an »Ilomantsi ax,» the eastern Finland form of the primitive ax. The axes were found in Harlu, Akaa, Ilomantsi, Kivijärvi, and Suomusjärvi.
NM 10210. 8 $^3/_8$ × 2 $^1/_2$ × 1 $^1/_2$ (209 × 63 × 38 mm.)
NM 2330:2. 9 $^9/_{16}$ × 3 $^7/_{16}$ × 1 $^3/_8$ (239 × 86 × 35 mm.)
NM 4433:1. 7 $^7/_8$ × 3 $^5/_8$ × 1 $^9/_{16}$ (196 × 91 × 39 mm.)
NM 2040:142. 6 $^1/_4$ × 3 $^3/_8$ × 1 $^1/_4$ (156 × 84 × 32 mm.)
NM 3801:2. 6 $^1/_{16}$ × 3 $^5/_{16}$ × $^{15}/_{16}$ (152 × 83 × 24 mm.)

4

Curved-back gouges of a type developed from the Ilomantsi type of ax. Most of them date from the Pre-Ceramic period, i.e., they are over 5,000 and possibly 7,000 years old. The gouges in the picture were found in Pusula, Metsäpirtti, and Sortavala(?).
NM 6650:1. 4 $^3/_{16}$ × 1 $^7/_8$ × 1 $^3/_{16}$ (117 × 47 × 30 mm.)
NM 7091:1. 5 $^3/_{16}$ × 1 $^1/_2$ × 1 $^1/_{16}$ (130 × 38 × 26 mm.)
NM 3420:4 6 $^{15}/_{16}$ × 1 $^3/_4$ × 1 $^3/_{16}$ (173 × 43 × 30 mm.)

5

Axes, gouges, and clubs from various periods of the Stone Age, mainly from the comb ceramics period (c. 3000 — 1700 B.C.). Found in Pusula, Kaukola, Hämeenkyrö, Alajärvi, Reisjärvi, Pielavesi, Porvoo, Metsäpirtti, Pernaja, Parikkala, Finnish or Russian Karelia, Sortavala, Suomusjärvi, Nousiainen, and Kaukola.
NM 6650:1. 4 $^{11}/_{16}$ × 1 $^7/_8$ × 1 $^3/_{16}$ (117 × 47 × 30 mm.)
NM 5929:2. 5 $^3/_8$ × 1 $^3/_8$ × $^{13}/_{16}$ (134 × 34 × 21 mm.)
NM 614. 4 × 3 $^1/_4$ × 1 $^3/_8$ (100 × 82 × 34 mm.)

NM 2907:3. 7 $^3/_8$ × 2 $^{15}/_{16}$ × $^1/_2$ (184 × 74 × 13 mm.)
NM 2477:36. 3 $^{11}/_{16}$ × 1 $^7/_{16}$ × $^{11}/_{16}$ (92 × 36 × 17 mm.)
NM 2023:5. Diameter 3 $^{13}/_{16}$ in. (95 mm.), width 1 $^3/_4$ in. (43 mm.)
NM 6083:1. 2 $^9/_{16}$ × $^{15}/_{16}$ × $^5/_8$ (64 × 24 × 15 mm.)
NM 7091:1. 5 $^3/_{16}$ × 1 $^1/_2$ × 1 $^1/_{16}$ (130 × 38 × 26 mm.)
NM 2346:29. 3 $^{13}/_{16}$ × 2 $^5/_{16}$ × $^3/_4$ (95 × 58 × 18 mm.)
NM 253. 6 $^5/_8$ × 1 $^3/_4$ × 1 $^1/_4$ (165 × 44 × 31 mm.)
NM 6767:4. 3 $^{13}/_{16}$ × $^{13}/_{16}$ × $^{11}/_{16}$ (96 × 20 × 17 mm.)
NM 3420:4. 6 $^{15}/_{16}$ × 1 $^3/_4$ × 1 $^3/_{16}$ (173 × 43 × 30 mm.)
NM 4166:4. 3 $^1/_4$ × 1 $^3/_4$ × $^5/_8$ (81 × 44 × 16 mm.)
NM 5650:2. 8 × 1 $^9/_{16}$ × 1 $^3/_8$ (200 × 39 × 34 mm.)
NM 7318. 4 $^5/_8$ × 1 $^3/_4$ × 1 $^1/_4$ (115 × 43 × 31 mm.)
NM 3089:68. 6 $^1/_{16}$ × 1 $^{13}/_{16}$ × 1 $^1/_2$ (152 × 46 × 37 mm.)

6

One round and two four-cornered perforated club stones, found in Alajärvi, Lapua, and Sakkola. The four-edged clubs are Pre-Ceramics, the round stone later, perhaps comb ceramics.
NM 2442:147. 6 $^9/_{16}$ × 5 $^{13}/_{16}$ × 1 $^3/_8$ (164 × 145 × 34 mm.)
NM 2443:198. 6 $^5/_8$ × 5 $^{13}/_{16}$ × 1 $^7/_{16}$ (166 × 145 × 36 mm.)
NM 5685:1. 4 $^7/_8$ × 4 $^1/_{16}$ × 1 $^5/_{16}$ (122 × 101 × 33 mm.)

7

Scored clubs. The ball-shaped club was found in Kiuruvesi, the flat stones in Punkalaidun and Kivijärvi. The former is Pre-Ceramics; the others are probably more recent.
NM 2540:1. 3 $^{11}/_{16}$ × 4 $^3/_8$ × 3 $^1/_4$ (92 × 110 × 81 mm.)
NM 2084:274. Diameter approx. 5 in. (125 — 127 mm.)
NM 3352:27. Diameter approx. 6 in. (134 — 163 mm.)

8

Two large and two small clay vessels over 4,000 years old. The big ones are decorated with indentations and comb stamping, hence the name »comb ceramics.» The comb ceramics culture in Finland dates from 3000 to 1700 B.C. The large vessels were found at Sätös in Kuusjärvi and Pennala in Orimattila, the small ones at Pere in Honkilahti and Tiurinmäki in Räisälä, places with Pre-Ceramic settlements. These were usually on sandy shore areas, which explains the strange tapered shape of the bottom — vessels shaped like this could be stood upright in sand.
NM 13060:57. Height 18 in. (450 mm.), diameter 16 $^{13}/_{16}$ in. (420 mm.)
NM 11196:539. Height 1 $^3/_4$ in. (44 mm.), diameter 3 $^1/_2$ in. (87 mm.)

NM 14697. Height 19 ⁵/₈ in. (490 mm.), diameter 18 ³/₈ in. (460 mm.)
NM 2789. Height 3 ¹³/₁₆ in. (95 mm.), diameter 3 ⁵/₈ in. (90 mm.)

9

A small clay cup from Pere, Honkilahti, decorated with comb stamp impressions.
NM 11196:538. Height 2 ³/₁₆ in. (55 mm.), diameter 4 ³/₈ in. (110 mm.)

10

Enlargement of the small clay drinking cup on the right in plate 8. The surface is attractively crisscrossed with rows of comb stampings.
NM 2789. Height 3 ¹³/₁₆ in. (95 mm.), diameter 3 ⁵/₈ in. (90 mm.)

11

Two small clay vessels reconstructed at the museum. The one on the left was found in Saunaniemi, Suonenjoki, the one on the right in Pere, Honkilahti. The former is decorated with comb stamping, the latter with small circles imprinted with a straw or reed.
NM 11810:1. Height 1 ¹³/₁₆ in. (45 mm.), diameter 3 ³/₁₆ in. (80 mm.)
NM 11196:539. Height 1 ³/₄ (44 mm.), diameter 3 ¹/₂ in. (87 mm.)

12

Clay vessel from Salo, Hankasalmi, decorated with alternate strips of large indentations and comb stamping. (See also plates 13 and 14.)
NM 3006:2. Height 13 ³/₁₆ in. (330 mm.), diameter 15 ³/₁₆ in. (380 mm.)

13

Rim from a clay vessel over 4,000 years old. The pieces were collected from a settlement in Kankaanlaita, Kerimäki, and have been dated as early comb ceramics.
NM 9055:3.

14

Reconstructed fragments of a large clay vessel decorated with indentations and comb stamping. The pieces are from Pääskylahti, Sääminki, and are about 4,000 years old.
NM 8787:108.

15

East Finland ceramics from Poventsa, East Karelia. The pieces, about 4,000 years old, date from the late comb ceramics period. Because of the rhombus-shaped imprint, this style of ceramics has been called »rhombic indentation ceramics.» It originated in eastern Europe and spread to the Karelian Isthmus around Lake Ladoga.
NM 11400:1.

16

Part of a large clay vessel, glued together from pieces of ceramics found in Pääskylahti, Sääminki, and dating back about 4,000 years.
NM 8690:4.

17

Four ice picks in tremolite-actinolite slate. This type of implement is the Far North's equivalent of the cradle-leg ax (plate 20). A large number of ice picks have been found in Rovaniemi, including three in the picture. The second from the right was found in Lapland. The first ice picks appeared at the end of the Pre-Ceramic period and remained unchanged until the end of the Stone Age.
NM 3266:12. Length 14 ⁵/₈ in. (365 mm.)
NM 10227:1. Length 16 ³/₈ in. (410 mm.)
NM 9339. Length 18 ¹¹/₁₆ in. (467 mm.)
NM 3266:21. Length 18 ³/₈ in. (460 mm.)

18

Picklike axes from Rovaniemi, between 4,000 and 5,000 years old.
NM 664. Length 14 ¹³/₁₆ in. (370 mm.)
NM 10736:1. Length 21 ³/₁₆ in. (530 mm.)

19

Scandinavian chisels from the comb ceramics period. The gouges on the left were found in Haapajärvi and Alajärvi, the flat chisels in Vehkalahti and Vesanto.
NM 3549:26. 3 ¹⁵/₁₆ × 2 ⁹/₁₆ × ⁹/₁₆ (98 × 64 × 14 mm.)
NM 2240:2. 10 ⁷/₁₆ × 3 ¹/₁₆ × ¹⁵/₆ (261 × 76 × 24 mm.)
NM 2907:3. 7 ³/₈ × 2 ¹⁵/₁₆ × ⁷/₁₆ (184 × 74 × 11 mm.)
NM 4035:1. 8 ³/₄ × 2 ¹¹/₁₆ × ⁵/₈ (219 × 67 × 16 mm.)

20

Cradle-leg-shaped picks and small chisels. The pick on the left was found in Sortavala, the other in Tohmajärvi. The small chisels are from the comb ceramics (3000 — 1700 B.C.) and Kiukainen culture (1600 — 1200 B.C.) periods. The one on the left, a »nail chisel», was found in Nurmo and possibly used as a scraper. The small flat chisel on the right was found in Piikkiö.
NM 11222. 17 ¹/₁₆ × 2 ⁷/₁₆ × 2 ¹/₂ (427 × 61 × 63 mm.)
NM 2814:10. 1 ¹³/₁₆ × 1 ³/₈ × ³/₈ (45 × 35 × 9 mm.)
NM 1991:6. 17 ⁵/₁₆ × 2 ⁷/₁₆ × 2 ⁵/₈ (433 × 61 × 65 mm.)
NM 5573:11. 2 ¹/₁₆ × 1 ¹/₂ × ⁵/₈ (52 × 38 × 15 mm.)

21

Ridge-backed gouge from Kiuruvesi, a real work of art made of green Onega slate. There is not a scratch on the piece, which would indicate that it was a sacrificial object and never actually used. It is between 4,000 and 5,000 years old.
NM 9914. 17 ¹/₁₆ × 1 ⁷/₁₆ × 1 ¹/₄ (427 × 36 × 32 mm.)

22

Two beautiful East Karelian chisels in green Onega slate. The flat chisel was found in Metsäpirtti, the gouge in Sahalahti. Such chisels date from the Pre-Ceramic period and were imported from Olonets.
NM 9181:3. 9 ¹³/₁₆ × 1 ³/₄ × 1 ⁵/₁₆ (246 × 43 × 33 mm.)
NM 2536:345. 9 ³/₈ × 1 ⁵/₈ × 1 ⁵/₁₆ (235 × 40 × 33 mm.)

23

Pronged clubs. The one on the far left was found in Pirtti-saari, Inari, and the indentations around the edge were perhaps for helving. The sandstone club in the middle is from Alavus and the tooth-edged one from Kuusamo. It is not known whether a toothed edge added to the weapon's efficiency or whether it was purely decorative.

NM 13291. $3^{13}/_{16} \times 3^{7}/_{16} \times 2^{1}/_{16}$ (96 × 86 × 52 mm.)
NM 2266:13. $5^{1}/_{4} \times 4^{3}/_{8} \times 1^{5}/_{8}$ (132 × 109 × 41 mm.)
NM 12098. $4^{7}/_{8} \times 4^{11}/_{16} \times 2^{13}/_{16}$ (122 × 117 × 70 mm.)

24

Tapered perforated weapon and cross-shaped clubs. The former represents the type of weapon common in western Finland at the end of the Pre-Ceramic period. The cross-shaped clubs were used as early as the Suomusjärvi culture period and remained in use until the end of the Stone Age. They have been found mostly in Satakunta and Ostrobothnia of present-day Finland, but they probably originated in Karelia. The perforated tapered weapon on the left was found on the Karelian Isthmus, the clubs in Keitele, Valkjärvi, and Impilahti.

NM 3805:4. $10^{1}/_{16} \times 3 \times 13/_{16}$ (252 × 75 × 21 mm.)
NM 2269. $13^{5}/_{8} \times 2^{11}/_{16} \times 1^{7}/_{8}$ (340 × 67 × 47 mm.)
NM 2159a. $10^{9}/_{16} \times 3^{3}/_{8} \times 1^{3}/_{4}$ (264 × 84 × 43 mm.)
NM 2916:12. $9^{5}/_{8} \times 2^{1}/_{4} \times 2^{11}/_{16}$ (241 × 57 × 67 mm.)

25

Slate armlets. Such ornaments were an effort to compensate for expensive imported amber jewelry. These were made in Finland even in the early comb ceramics period, about 5,000 years ago.

NM 2770:7.   NM 3769:2.
NM 9428:2.   NM 10867:30.
NM 2657:3
Copy
Maximum diameter $4^{3}/_{16}$ in. (105 mm.),
minimum $1^{3}/_{16}$ in. (30 mm.)

26

Amber jewelry from the comb ceramics period. The unique pendant decorated with a human face was found in Metsäpirtti; the other ornaments are from Muolaa, Evijärvi, Yli-Ii, Kalvola, Sakkola, Lapua, and Viipuri. With one exception, the amber found in Finland was imported from eastern Prussia, which was an amber-trading center.

NM 2840. $1^{7}/_{16} \times 1^{5}/_{16} \times 1/_{2}$ (36 × 33 × 12 mm.)
NM 3922:2. $15/_{16} \times 13/_{16} \times 5/_{8}$ (23 × 20 × 9 mm.)
NM 14396. $1^{1}/_{8} \times 1/_{2} \times 1/_{2}$ (28 × 12 × 12 mm.)
NM 1922:392. $2^{1}/_{8} \times 7/_{8} \times 3/_{8}$ (53 × 22 × 10 mm.)
NM 10415. $2 \times 1^{1}/_{4} \times 1/_{4}$ (50 × 32 × 6 mm.)
NM 6195:2. $1^{1}/_{16} \times 15/_{16} \times 7/_{16}$ (26 × 23 × 11 mm.)
NM 4302:15. $1^{1}/_{2} \times 1^{3}/_{8} \times 1/_{4}$ (37 × 34 × 6 mm.)
NM 5713:7. $2 \times 1 \times 3/_{8}$ (50 × 25 × 10 mm.)

27

Spearhead from Utsjoki. Possibly eastern European flint, which was imported into Finland in large quantities

during the comb ceramics period (3000 — 1700 B.C.).
NM 8834. $9^{3}/_{16} \times 2^{7}/_{16} \times 1/_{2}$ (230 × 61 × 13 mm.)

28

Arrowheads from various Stone Age periods. The long dark arrowhead is slate and was found in Ilomantsi; the saw-edged head is quartz and from Alahärmä; the others are flint, imported 4,000 — 4,200 years ago. The flint arrowheads were found in Ilomantsi, Ruotsinpyhtää, the Helsinki region, and Uskela.

NM 7172:1. $1^{5}/_{8} \times 3/_{8} \times 1/_{8}$ (40 × 10 × 3 mm.)
NM 11606. $3^{1}/_{4} \times 5/_{8} \times 3/_{16}$ (82 × 15 × 4 mm.)
NM 10498:2. $1^{9}/_{16} \times 1/_{2} \times 3/_{16}$ (39 × 13 × 5 mm.)
NM 11283. $2^{1}/_{16} \times 3/_{4} \times 3/_{8}$ (52 × 19 × 9 mm.)
NM 5668:4. $4^{7}/_{16} \times 7/_{16} \times 7/_{16}$ (111 × 11 × 11 mm.)
NM 7817. $3^{9}/_{16} \times 1/_{2} \times 1/_{4}$ (89 × 13 × 7 mm.)

29

Stone-headed arrows from Kodiak Island. The helving method used by the Kodiaks to attach heads to their arrows was possibly known as early as the Finnish Stone Age.
NM exotica collection: 102(b):6 and 121.

30

T-shaped slate implements, possibly used for cutting skins. The lower one has a clear resemblance to an animal, a fox or wolf. Both were found in Pitkämäki, Lapua, and date from 2000 — 1700 B.C., the end of the comb ceramics period.

NM 13048. $4^{3}/_{16} \times 2^{9}/_{16} \times 3/_{8}$(105 × 64 × 10 mm.)
NM 14117:1. $3^{15}/_{16} \times 2^{3}/_{16} \times 1/_{4}$ (99 × 54 × 6 mm.)

31

Harpoon heads. The larger head was found in Oulunjoki and is made of elk bone; the shorter one is from Muolaa. Judging by the peat stratification, the Oulunjoki harpoon is typical comb ceramics, i.e., about 4,000 years old.

NM 10310:1. $9^{7}/_{16} \times 1/_{4} \times 3/_{8}$ (236 × 24 × 10 mm.)
NM 9573:5. $5^{1}/_{16} \times 15/_{16} \times 1/_{4}$ (126 × 24 × 7 mm.)

32

Pine carving of elk's head from Lehtojärvi, Rovaniemi. The surface layers of the carving reveal remains of red ochre. The carving has been assigned to the Litorina period, possibly very early, which would make it as much as 7,000 years old and thus one of Finland's oldest sculptures.

NM 14189. $15^{5}/_{8} \times 4^{3}/_{8} \times 3$ (390 × 110 × 75 mm.)

33

Pine carving from Pohja. Between 4,000 and 5,000 years old, it is thought to have been connected with a cult, as the face has been smeared with grease, blood, or some other substance that has prevented rotting.

NM 3481:1. $9^{13}/_{16} \times 3^{13}/_{16} \times 2^{1}/_{4}$ (245 × 95 × 56 mm.)

34

Spoon with duck's head handle from Viekki, Pielisjärvi, carved from Siberian cembra pine and probably brought to Finland by traders. The spoon's age is uncertain, but it could be comb ceramics and thus over 4,000 years old.
NM 9003. $5\,^5/_{16} \times 3\,^1/_8 \times 1\,^1/_4$ ($133 \times 78 \times 31$ mm.)

35

Elk's head spoon from Kittilä and bear's head spoon from Laukaa. The former is made of Finnish pine and has been ascribed to the Bronze Age, but it may be even more recent. The latter is of Siberian cembra pine and was probably imported. It may be comb ceramics.
NM 10179. $8\,^3/_{16} \times 2\,^1/_2$ (205×63 mm.)
NM 6321. $10\,^1/_2 \times 2\,^{13}/_{16}$ (262×70 mm.)

36

Stone knob-ended hammer axes, copies of copper axes. The ax on the left was found in Kemijärvi, but was originally from eastern Russia and is over 4,000 years old. The multi-edged hammer ax on the right, roughly the same age, was found in Hämeenniemi, Lapua, but originally imported from Scandinavia.
NM 2565. $8\,^5/_8 \times 2\,^1/_2 \times 2\,^1/_{16}$ ($216 \times 62 \times 51$ mm.)
NM 10225. $6\,^3/_8 \times 1\,^7/_8 \times 1\,^5/_8$ ($160 \times 47 \times 40$ mm.)

37

Swedish boat-shaped ax. Found in Nurmijärvi, the ax is made of extremely fine diabase and was imported from Sweden about 1800 B.C.
NM 9781. $1\,^9/_{16} \times 2\,^1/_4 \times 1\,^3/_8$ ($157 \times 56 \times 35$ mm.)

38

Boat-shaped hammer axes about 3,700 years old. They are made of Satakunta olivine diabase and are basically Finnish in design. The axes were found in Nurmo, Paimio (2), Lieto, and Sääksmäki.
NM 1013. $7\,^{13}/_{16} \times 2\,^9/_{16} \times 1\,^1/_2$ ($183 \times 64 \times 38$ mm.)
NM 9080. $7\,^{11}/_{16} \times 2\,^3/_4 \times 1\,^7/_8$ ($192 \times 68 \times 47$ mm.)
NM 1858. $7\,^7/_8 \times 2\,^5/_8 \times 1\,^1/_2$ ($197 \times 65 \times 38$ mm.)
NM 6566:1. $8\,^3/_{16} \times 2\,^3/_8 \times 1\,^5/_8$ ($205 \times 60 \times 40$ mm.)
NM 1137. $8\,^1/_4 \times 2\,^{15}/_{16} \times 1\,^{15}/_{16}$ ($206 \times 73 \times 48$ mm.)

39

Three shouldered axes. They belong to the Hammer Ax culture and were found in Vihanti, Teuva, and Urjala.
NM 12213. $7\,^3/_4 \times 2\,^3/_8 \times 1\,^7/_8$ ($194 \times 60 \times 47$ mm.)
NM 9049. $9\,^1/_2 \times 2\,^9/_{16} \times 2\,^1/_8$ ($238 \times 64 \times 53$ mm.)
NM 6673:9. $7\,^3/_8 \times 2\,^5/_{16} \times 2$ ($184 \times 58 \times 50$ mm.)

40

Four-sided working Ax from the Hammer Ax period, found in Virolahti, and a late Stone Age gouge from Ruotsinpyhtää.
NM 2453:25. $7\,^7/_{16} \times 2\,^5/_8 \times 1\,^7/_8$ ($186 \times 65 \times 47$ mm.)
NM 2346:127. $5\,^1/_2 \times 2\,^1/_4 \times 1\,^3/_8$ ($137 \times 56 \times 35$ mm.)

41

Twine ceramics from the Hammer Ax culture (2000—1600

B.C.). The small bowls in the foreground and the large one on the right are from the Eknäs grave in Porvoo, the large bowl on the left is from Tammenmäki, Kaarina, and the little drinking cup in the middle is from Luokankangas, Pirttikylä.
NM 14163:7. Height $2\,^5/_8$ in. (66 mm.), diameter $3\,^1/_8$ in. (78 mm.)
NM 11149. Height $2\,^{13}/_{16}$ in. (71 mm.), diameter $4\,^1/_{16}$ in. 102 mm.)
NM 14163:11. Height $6\,^1/_4$ in. (157 mm.), diameter $5\,^7/_8$ in. (147 mm.)
NM 13112:3. Height $6\,^5/_8$ in. (170 mm.), diameter $6\,^3/_8$ in. (160 mm.)
NM 14163:6. Height $2\,^5/_8$ in. (66 mm.), diameter $3\,^3/_{16}$ in. (79 mm.)

42

Grindstones found in Tapanila, Helsinki. The base stone is granite and the grinder gneiss. A shouldered ax found near the grindstones would indicate the Hammer Ax period (2000—1600 B.C.).
NM 13425:1. $23 \times 16\,^3/_8 \times 6$ ($575 \times 410 \times 150$ mm.)
NM 13425:2. $9\,^1/_4 \times 6\,^5/_8 \times 3\,^3/_{16}$ ($231 \times 164 \times 79$ mm.)

43

Clay idols from Åland, found at the Jettböle settlement at Jomala. They are thought to have been cult objects and are about 3,700 years old.
NM 8320:23. $1\,^1/_{16} \times 1\,^1/_{16}$ (26×26 mm.)
NM 4782:471. $1\,^3/_4 \times 1\,^5/_{16}$ (44×33 mm.)

44

Clay image from the Jettböle settlement in Åland, about 3,700 years old. The decoration on the body is thought to represent clothing. The scorings on the face have been interpreted as a beard and hair or as tattoo marks.
NM 5180:57, 4782:451. $4 + 1\,^5/_8 \times 1\,^3/_4 \times 1\,^3/_{16}$ ($100 + 40 \times 43 \times 30$ mm.)

45 and 46

»The old man of Rovaniemi,» in gray stone, was found at a Stone Age settlement in Niska, Rovaniemi. The site was still occupied during the Hammer Ax culture period.
NM 14699:3158. $2\,^1/_{16} \times \,^4/_8 \times \,^{13}/_{16}$ ($51 \times 16 \times 21$ mm.)

47

Ax representing a man from Kiuruvesi, the only one of its kind in Europe. The stone is uralite porphyry, and in shape the weapon is reminiscent of Neolithic perforated axes, though no exact equivalent has been found. It is about 3,500 years old.
NM 11708. $6\,^5/_{16} \times 2\,^5/_8 \times 1\,^5/_8$ ($158 \times 66 \times 41$ mm.)

48 and 49

The Huittinen elk's head club. This soapstone piece may be as much as 5,000 years old and is thus Finland's oldest animal-head weapon.
NM 6292. $5\,^7/_8 \times 2\,^5/_{16} \times 2\,^5/_{16}$ ($147 \times 58 \times 74$ mm.)

50

Elk's head club found in Espoo. The club is of gneiss and is probably about 3,500 years old.
NM 2611. $8 \times 7 \times 1\,^{15}/_{16}$ (200 × 175 × 48 mm.)

51

The main part of a perforated weapon decorated with an elk's head, made out of fine East Karelian tuff. The piece was found in Säkkijärvi and has been identified as Neolithic.
NM 4909:1. $5\,^1/_4 \times 1\,^5/_8 \times 1\,^5/_8$ (132 × 41 × 41 mm.)

52

Perforated ax carved of soapstone, decorated with a bear's head. Found in Antrea, the ax is perhaps 3,600 to 3,800 years old.
NM 1557. $9 \times 2\,^3/_8 \times 1\,^1/_2$ (225 × 60 × 38 mm.)

53

The Paltamo bear's head chopper, made of soapstone and probably between 3,500 and 3,800 years old.
NM 13275:1. $7\,^5/_8 \times 1\,^5/_8 \times 1\,^3/_4$ (191 × 41 × 43 mm.)

54

The fore-end of a sleigh runner, finished off with an animal head. The piece was found in a marsh at Ketlahti, Heinola, and is probably Neolithic.
NM 12923:1. Width $5\,^3/_{16}$ in. (130 mm.)

55

Knife in Rovaniemi red slate decorated with an elk's head. The knife is believed to date from the Hammer Ax period and was probably imported from Scandinavia.
NM 9972:1. $3\,^3/_8 \times 1\,^1/_{16} \times ^1/_4$ (85 × 26 × 6 mm.)

56

Red slate knives from the end of the Stone Age (c. 1500 B.C.). The curved knife ending in a bird's head was found in Sodankylä, the bear's head knife in Pyhäjoki. Both were probably imported from red slate areas in Scandinavia.
NM 15000. $6\,^{13}/_{16} \times 1\,^5/_8 \times ^1/_4$ (170 × 40 × 6 mm.)
NM 13438. $6\,^3/_8 \times 1\,^1/_{16} \times ^3/_8$ (160 × 27 × 9 mm.)

57

Three barbed spearheads, found in Utajärvi, Rovaniemi, and Muhos. The one on the left is grayish stone, the others red slate, and all were probably imported from Scandinavia about 4,000 years ago.
NM 3045:18. $4\,^{13}/_{16} \times 1\,^1/_4 \times ^3/_8$ (120 × 32 × 9 mm.)
NM 9260:1. $4\,^1/_2 \times 1\,^1/_4 \times ^5/_{16}$ (112 × 32 × 8 mm.)
NM 8237. $6\,^{13}/_{16} \times 1\,^3/_8 \times ^3/_8$ (170 × 34 × 9 mm.)

58

Pieces imported from Scandinavia, a flint dagger and what are called »saws,» although they were certainly not used as such. The dagger, lowest in the picture, was found in Huittinen, the »saws» in Halikko, Espoo, and Piikkiö. All are probably about 3,500 years old.

NM 4113. $5\,^5/_8 \times 1\,^7/_{16} \times ^3/_8$ (140 × 36 × 9 mm.)
NM 6927:1. $6\,^3/_{16} \times 1\,^1/_4 \times ^3/_8$ (155 × 31 × 10 mm.)
NM 5970:621. $6\,^1/_{16} \times 1\,^1/_2 \times 3\,^5/_8$ (152 × 38 × 20 mm.)
NM 3696:1 $6\,^9/_{16} \times 1\,^3/_4 \times ^1/_2$ (164 × 44 × 12 mm.)

59

Flint weapons from the end of the Stone Age (c. 1500 B.C.), probably imported from Scandinavia. The dagger with a hilt was found in Pori, the others in Halikko, Espoo, and Piikkiö.
NM 6927:1. $6\,^3/_{16} \times 1\,^1/_4 \times ^3/_8$ (155 × 31 × 10 mm.)
NM 4113. $5\,^5/_8 \times 1\,^7/_{16} \times ^3/_8$ (140 × 36 × 9 mm.)
NM 145. $7\,^1/_2 \times 2\,^1/_{16} \times ^1/_2$ (188 × 52 × 13 mm.)
NM 3696:1 $6\,^9/_{16} \times 1\,^3/_4 \times ^1/_2$ (164 × 44 × 12 mm.)

60

Late perforated axes. The one on the far left was found outside Helsinki and is a »flat-backed perforated ax.» This type has been found mainly in eastern Russia. The one at the front is a typical »rhombic ax,» found in Enontekiö. Near it in form is the porphyry perforated ax, upper right, found in Sammatti. The ax on the far right is an eastern import and was found in Tiuri, Räisälä. The axes from the east are Neolithic, the rhombic axes Bronze Age.
NM 6190:8. $4\,^{11}/_{16} \times 1\,^7/_{16} \times 1\,^{11}/_{16}$ (117 × 36 × 42 mm.)
NM 9453. $3\,^{13}/_{16} \times 2\,^3/_{16} \times 1\,^7/_8$ (95 × 55 × 47 mm.)
NM 8762. $3\,^7/_{16} \times 2 \times 1\,^1/_2$ (86 × 50 × 38 mm.)
NM 9074. $3\,^{11}/_{16} \times 2\,^3/_{16} \times 1\,^5/_8$ (92 × 55 × 40 mm.)

61

Two beautifully decorated shouldered axes over 3,000 years old, from the late Bronze Age. The pieces were found together in Helsinki and are thought to have been made in southern Scandinavia.
NM 72. Length $9\,^3/_{16}$ in. (230 mm.) and $9\,^1/_2$ in. (237 mm.)

62

Two cast-bronze shouldered axes and a celt, found in Dragsfjärd, Uskela, and Kemiö. All these tools are northern European in design, and their nearest equivalents are found in Sweden. The shouldered axes date back about 3,000 years, the celt from perhaps 350 years later.
NM 1910. Length $5\,^{13}/_{16}$ in. (145 mm.)
NM 800. Length $4\,^1/_{16}$ in. (102 mm.)
NM 9305. Length $6\,^3/_4$ in. (168 mm.)

63

Two bronze celts, ascribed to c. 800—700 B.C. They were found in Maaninka and Paimio and are of the »Maaninka» type, a Finnish variation of the celt.
NM 5311. Length $4\,^1/_{16}$ in. (101 mm.)
NM 10454. Length $4\,^1/_{16}$ in. (101 mm.)

64

Bronze Age casting molds, the one on the left from Valimo, the one on the right from Ylitornio. The molds are of soapstone, made for casting celts similar to the

eastern European Ananjino type, and are probably about 2,500 years old.
NM 13934. 2 ³/₄ × 2 ¹/₂ × ³/₈ (68 × 62 × 10 mm.)
NM 2160. 3 ⁵/₁₆ × 2 ¹/₄ × 1 ¹/₁₆ (83 × 57 × 26 mm.)

65

The »Möriger» sword, found in Kokemäki. The weapon is about 2,600 years old and was possibly brought to Finland from Hungary.
NM 2791:1. Length 28 ⁵/₈ in. (715 mm.)

66

Bronze Age sword hilts. The one in the foreground illustrates the fashion about 2,600 years ago, the two others are 500 or 600 years older. The hilts belong to swords found in Kokemäki, Dragsfjärd, and Kiukainen.
NM 2791:1.   NM 2503:A:1.   NM 13770.

67

Bronze Age spearhead from Uskela and a dagger from Dragsfjärd. The dagger is early Bronze Age, about 1300–1200 B.C., the spearhead late Bronze Age and thus 300 to 500 years more recent. Both are probably Scandinavian.
NM 7109. Length 11 in. (275 mm.)
NM 2503:A:1. Length 10 ⁵/₁₆ in. (258 mm.)

68

A snow scraper made of reindeer antler found in Tyrväntö during a dredging of the Lepaa River. From earth samples, the piece has been ascribed to the Bronze Age and is thought to be 3,000 years old.
NM 145000. Length 15 ³/₁₆ in. (380 mm.)

69

Three bronze »eyeglass» buckles found in Kokemäki, the two at the top in the village of Kuoppala, the third on the Noppari farm in Ylistaro village. The buckles are a type familiar in Scandinavia and are about 2,500 years old.
NM 10732:2. Length 6 ¹⁵/₁₆ in. (174 mm.)
NM 2791:2. Length 11 ⁵/₈ in. (290 mm.)
NM 10732:1. Length 10 ³/₁₆ in. (254 mm.)

70

A bronze sword and three bronze necklets which were found in Kiukainen, in the village of Panelia. The sword was found alone, the three necklets together, and they are thought to have been sacrificial. The sword is about 3,000 to 3,200 years old, the necklets from about 500 years later, and already Bronze/Iron Age. The sword probably reached Finland from southern Germany or the Danube area; the necklets may be from central Sweden.
NM 13770. Length 24 ³/₈ in. (610 mm.)
NM 2476. Diameter 8 in. (200 mm.),
8 ¹/₄ in. (207 mm.), and 10 in. (250 mm.)

71

Iron weapons and tools from the Pernaja find, which is

thought to have been the cache of some foreign merchant. The Finns who moved into the country after the birth of Christ, and who thus came under the influence of the Iron Age culture of the Finnish peninsula, used sickles, working axes, and spear blades of this type.
NM 12130.

72

Boss and hold from a beautiful decorative shield, a unique import that was perhaps made in Bohemia around A.D. 100. The pieces are bronze, partly silver plate, and were found at the Koskenhaka burial ground in Piikkiö.
NM 10605:83. 5 ⁵/₁₆ × 4 ⁹/₁₆ × 4 ⁹/₁₆ (133 × 114 × 114 mm.)
NM 10605:84. Length 7 ⁵/₈ in. (190 mm.)

73

Bronze bracelets from Kroggårdsmalm in Karjaa. The bracelet on the left is made of 27 separate rings; the other is an even strip of bronze twisted into a spiral. The ornaments date back to A.D. 200 or earlier.
NM 10612:10.   NM 9535:1.

74

Bronze necklet with horn-shaped ends of a type worn by the Finns in the early centuries A.D. The piece was found in Piikkiö.
NM 10547:1. Diameter 7 ¹/₄–9 ¹/₈ (193–228 mm.)

75

Roman wine stoup found in Perkiö, Vähäkyrö, from the first century A.D. The stoup bears the imprint of L. Ansius Diodorus of Capua.
NM 1453. 9 ⁵/₈ × 5 ³/₁₆ × 2 ¹/₂ (241 × 130 × 62 mm.)

76

Glass drinking horn found at Laitila, which the museum has glued together from over 100 pieces. The horn is from c. A.D. 300 and was made somewhere on the Rhine.
NM 13200:5. Height 11 ³/₈ in. (285 mm.), diameter of mouth 4 ³/₄ in. (118 mm.)

77 and 78

Horseshoe buckle decorated in enamel. Although this piece was found in Nokia, such buckles were more likely made in Virumaa and date back to the fourth century A.D.
NM 8897. Diameter 4 ⁹/₁₆ in. (114 mm.)

79

Bronze spring clasps. The clasp decorated with rings was found in Köönikänmäki, Kokemäki, and is from c. A.D. 500. The other, called a »spade-foot clasp», was found in Urjala and belongs to roughly the same period. Both may have been made in the eastern Baltic.
NM 3988:22. 4 ⁵/₁₆ × 3 ¹⁵/₁₆ (108 × 98 mm.)
NM 2505:17. 3 ¹⁵/₁₆ × 2 ¹/₄ (98 × 56 mm.)

80

Gold jewelry from the Old Iron Age. The necklet with animal-head ends, dated at A.D. 200, is a copy of one found in Nousiainen in 1770 and now in Stockholm. The other necklet fragments and the ring in the same design are from Uskela and date from about A.D. 300. All were probably imported from Scandinavia. The plain ring decorated with lines around the edge is from the following century and is the only one of its kind in Finland; it was found in Vähäkyrö.

NM 6450:4,15.
NM 1110:6. Diameter $^{13}/_{16}$ in. (21 mm.)
NM 6658:40. Diameter $^{15}/_{16}$ in. (23 mm.) National History Museum, Stockholm. Diameter 6 $^{13}/_{16}$ — 7 $^{1}/_{4}$ (171—182 mm.)

81

Top, bronze buckle from the later Roman Iron Age (A.D. 200—400) and a spiral ring. Below, two branched clasps that were used at that time, in southern Ostrobothnia in particular; the ones in the photograph are from Laihia. The clasp with a triple »foot» is also from Laihia and is unique of its type in Finland. The triple-foot clasp was decorated with pieces of silver that have since fallen off. It was found in Vähäkyrö and is probably sixth century A.D. Spiral rings were used throughout the Iron Age; the one in the picture, from the same period as the branched clasps, was found in Mujanvainio, Laihia.

NM 10856:10. Length 2 $^{5}/_{8}$ in. (65 mm.)
NM 10856:8. Length 2 in. (50 mm.)
NM 10621:1. Length 2 $^{7}/_{8}$ in. (72 mm.)
NM 9066:36. Length 4 $^{5}/_{8}$ in. (116 mm.)
NM 10621:3. Diameter $^{13}/_{16}$ in. (20 mm.)

82

Large flat silver clasp partly gilded and niello-decorated and covered with animal ornamentation. The clasp was found in Tytärsaari and is Swedish, made in the sixth century A.D.

NM 3382:1. Length 6 $^{13}/_{16}$ in. (170 mm.)

83

Bronze belt buckle and mountings found in Tytärsaari and decorated with human heads. They may have been imported from Sweden and date from A.D. 400 to 600.

NM 8703:1. Length 3 $^{7}/_{16}$ in. (86 mm.)
NM 8703:3. Length $^{15}/_{16}$ in. (23 mm.)
NM 8703:6. Length $^{15}/_{16}$ in. (24 mm.)
NM 8703:4. Length $^{13}/_{16}$ in. (20 mm.)

84

Weapons from the early migratory period. The shield boss was found in Tenhola, the sword and spearheads in Kokemäki. The weapons in the picture are typical arms of a soldier of the period—sword, spear, and shield—which also accompanied him on his journey to the next world. Swords were often bent in two (as in the picture) or coiled (plate 104) so that they could not be used from beyond the grave to hurt the living. Sometimes the other weapons were also rendered harmless. Usually, only the iron bosses that protected the hand and a few rivets and supports have been preserved from the shields, which were of leather or wood.

NM 2905. Height 4 $^{1}/_{2}$ in. (112 mm.), diameter 5 $^{11}/_{16}$ in. (142 mm.)
NM 2377:4. Length 11 $^{7}/_{8}$ in. (297 mm.)
NM 2377:2. Length 15 $^{1}/_{16}$ in. (376 mm.)
NM 2377:5. Length 35 $^{3}/_{8}$ in. (885 mm.)
NM 2377:3. Length 11 $^{3}/_{4}$ in. (294 mm.)

85

Iron shield bosses from the period of the Great Migration (A.D. 400—800). The ones on the far right, found in Tenhola, is the oldest. The typical Finnish boss, in the backround, dates from A.D. 550—650 and was found in the same place. The »Vandal type» boss, on the left, is from the same period and was found in Kalanti, and the round boss from Laitila, in the foreground, is the most recent, dating from the late seventh or eighth century.

NM 2421:15. Height 3 $^{13}/_{16}$ in. (95 mm.), diameter 4 $^{9}/_{16}$ in. (114 mm.)
NM 11214:4. Height 5 $^{1}/_{16}$ in. (126 mm.), diameter 6 $^{15}/_{16}$ in. (173 mm.)
NM 5552:9. Height 5 $^{3}/_{16}$ in. (130 mm.), diameter 5 $^{3}/_{16}$ in. (130 mm.)
NM 2905. Height 4 $^{1}/_{2}$ in. (112 mm.), diameter 5 $^{11}/_{16}$ in. (142 mm.)

86

This bronze clasp from Maalahti is a Finnish adaptation of the ring-decorated clasp; raised ridges are used in place of the rings. This form of decoration may have developed in southern Ostrobothnia in A.D. 450—550.

NM 4263:8. 4 $^{13}/_{16}$ × 3 $^{3}/_{16}$ (120 × 80 mm.)

87

A belt buckle decorated with animal ornamentation, found in Gulldynt, Vöyri, and the only one of its type in Finland. It was almost certainly imported and dates from A.D. 400—600.

NM 8515. 2 $^{5}/_{16}$ × 2 $^{1}/_{16}$ (58 × 51 mm.)

88

Snake clasps. The snake clasp perhaps originated in Gotland, but appealed to Finnish taste so much that it appears in Finland much more than in Sweden and was also made in Finland. The clasps are from the seventh and eighth centuries A.D. and are always made of bronze.

NM 8615:1. 3 $^{1}/_{4}$ × 2 $^{3}/_{16}$ (81 × 54 mm.)
NM 2001c:2. 3 $^{3}/_{8}$ × 2 $^{1}/_{8}$ (84 × 53 mm.)
NM 2441:3. 3 $^{1}/_{16}$ × 2 $^{1}/_{8}$ (77 × 53 mm.)

89

Single-animal snake clasp found in Gulldynt, Vöyri. The snake's tail is also shaped like a head.

NM 8562:1. 3 $^{1}/_{16}$ × 2 $^{1}/_{8}$ (76 × 53 mm.)

90

Two round punched clasps found in Kalanti and Laitila. This type of clasp comes from the Memel area and was worn around the year 800.

NM 9365:450. Diameter 3 $\frac{1}{16}$ in. (62 mm.)
NM 2548:694. Diameter 2 $\frac{3}{8}$ in. (59 mm.)

91

Ornamental pins from the end of the migratory period, i.e., about 800. The Y-shaped pin is from Korkenoja, Raisio, the ring-shaped one from Mustamäki, Halikko. The pins were used to fasten a cloak and are found mainly in Finland and the eastern Baltic. The one on the left is probably originally Latvian; the one on the right is an Estonian type.
NM 12192. Length 10 $\frac{3}{8}$ in. (259 mm.)
NM 5512:39. Length 7 in. (175 mm.)

92

Bronze chains from Nastola dating from the 8th century. Chains like these were the finest ornamentation of a woman's dress in the later migratory period. They were hung across the breast and attached at the shoulders with the end fasteners.
NM 12000:1. Length 37 $\frac{3}{16}$ in. (930 mm.)

93

Ornamental chains similar to the one in plate 92. The three in this picture were found complete in Kuhmoinen, Nastola, and Janakkala and are examples of the fashion in jewelry around 800.
NM 12000:1.   NM 7854:9.
NM 14530:1.

94

A bronze circular clasp and chain, from about 800. The piece was found in Lukkarinmäki, Uskela, and is of a type common around the Oka River in central Russia.
NM 9192:1. Diameter 2 $\frac{3}{16}$ in. (55 mm.)

95

A bronze comb-edge pendant from the Papinsaari treasure trove, Kuhmoinen, dating from c. 800.
NM 7854:8. 2 × 1 $\frac{9}{16}$ (50 × 39 mm.)

96

A bronze mounting found in Hattelmala, Hämeenlinna, and dating from A.D. 600—800. The mounting is decorated with animal ornamentation and was probably imported from Sweden.
NM 8615:9. 2 $\frac{3}{8}$ × 2 (59 × 50 mm.)

97

A bronze chain holder from Kernaala, Janakkala. The piece is unique, and from other ornaments in the same find it has been dated at about 800.
NM 14530:3. 2 $\frac{7}{8}$ × 2 $\frac{3}{4}$ × $\frac{1}{8}$ (72 × 68 × 3 mm.)

98

Pendants from around 800. The one on the left is the »Thor's Hammer» pendant, that on the right a comb-edged pendant, and the one in the middle a round punched-out pendant with two birds bill to bill. The pendants were found in Papinsaari, Kuhmoinen.
NM 7854:7 a—c.

99

Beads from the later migratory period (A.D. 600—800.) The beads are solid glass and were found in Kaparkullen, Vöyri. Simple types of beads may have been made in Scandinavia, but more decorated beads were probably imported from central or southern Europe.
NM 15.   NM 2910:1.   NM 2891:15.

100

Finnish clasp designs from the later migratory period, based on Swedish models. The clasp on the right and the crayfish-shaped clasp in the middle were found in Vesilahti. The other crayfish clasp is from Kalanti.
NM 8912:561. Length 2 $\frac{1}{16}$ in. (52 mm.)
NM 5165:23. Length 1 $\frac{3}{4}$ in. (44 mm.)
NM 5165:28. Length 2 $\frac{1}{4}$ in. (56 mm.)

101

Long, barbed Merovingian-type spears from the later migratory period, when purely Finnish designs developed. Such spears were very popular weapons at that time. The spears in the picture were found in Vehmaa, Kokemäki, and Vesilahti.
NM 2022:6. Length 19 $\frac{13}{16}$ in. (495 mm.)
NM 9249:71. Length 24 $\frac{11}{16}$ in. (617 mm.)
NM 5578:27. Length 41 $\frac{3}{16}$ in. (1,030 mm.)

102

The hilt of a rich sword found in Pappilanmäki, Eura. The pommel and deflector are silver-plated and gilded bronze decorated with animal and plaited ornamentation. The handle is wood. The hilt is late seventh century and possibly Finnish-made.
NM 11002:5. Hilt length 6 in. (150 mm.)

103 and 104

Iron sword with bronze hilt from Ristimäki, Kaarina, which dates from sometime between the migratory period and the Viking period, i.e., c. 800; it was possibly made in Gotland. The hilt is decorated with Scandinavian ornamentation, the main motifs being the bird and lion patterns in the ovals.
NM 6753:1, 6969:23. Length 36 in. (900 mm.)

105

Razor and fire steels. The razor is from Kärsämäki, Maaria, and dates back to the early migratory period (A.D. 400—600). The fire steels were found in Kangasala, Kokemäki, and Huittinen and are from the Viking period.
NM 2001:52. 2 $\frac{3}{4}$ × 2 $\frac{1}{16}$ (68 × 51 mm.)
NM 12882:308. 3 $\frac{3}{4}$ × $\frac{11}{16}$ (94 × 17 mm.)
NM 5869:6. 3 $\frac{1}{8}$ × 1 $\frac{1}{2}$ (78 × 38 mm.)
NM 3149:18. 3 × $\frac{15}{16}$ (75 × 24 mm.)

106

Iron Age hunting and fishing implements. The forklike arrowhead was found in Enontekiö, the barbed one in Laukaa, and the fish spear in Loppi. The small arrowhead is from the later migratory period; the others are

perhaps from the Viking period.
NM 10433. Length 7 in. (175 mm.)
NM 3426. 6 1/2 × 2 15/16 (163 × 73 mm.)
NM 8993. Length 4 1/4 in. (106 mm.)

107

Battle-ax or hatchet and a spearhead from the eleventh century. The ax was found in Vesilahti, the spearhead in Osmanmäki, Eura.
NM 3973:2. 8 3/8 × 7 7/8 (209 × 197 mm.)
NM 4633:15. Length 15 5/8 in. (380 mm.)

108

Three Viking spearheads from the eleventh century. The top one, the socket decorated with inlaid silver thread, was found in Suomela, Vesilahti; the middle one is from Kurkijoki and the bottom one from Sakkola.
NM 3010:21. Length 12 5/8 in. (315 mm.)
NM 8800:1. Length 17 3/16 in. (430 mm.)
NM 7625:1. Length 25 in. (625 mm.)

109

Silver-ornamented spearhead sockets from the eleventh century. The two on the left are decorated in the runic animal style, and the one on the right (the only one of its kind in Finland) in Ringerik style. The heads were found in Rapola, Sääksmäki, in Leikkimäki, Kokemäki, and in Laukko, Vesilahti, and were probably imported from Gotland.
NM 1063.   NM 1174:8.   NM 439.

110

Sword hilts from the later Iron Age. The sword on the far left is from the end of the migratory period, the next two are from the Viking period (800—1050), and the two bronze hilts on the right are from the time of the Crusades (1050—1300). The swords were found in Tiikkinummi, Perniö, in Taskula, Maaria, in Hukari, Vesilahti, in Kekomäki, Kaukola, and in Kiviniemi, Sakkola.
NM 7752:37.   NM 10842:39.
NM 2886:11.   NM 2595:75.
NM 7810.

111

Bronze scales case found in Hiisimäki, Märttelä Rusko, and dating from the Viking period. Merchants used delicate bronze scales for weighing silver coin, and graves where such scales have been found can be considered those of traders.
NM 7452:5. Diameter 4 3/16 in. (105 mm.), height 2 15/16 in. (73 mm.)

112

Bronze pot found in Bertby, Saltvik. When found, the pot contained 800 pieces of Arabian silver money, the most recent stamped A.D. 890. The pot is eastern and the top is marked with characters as well as other ornamentation. It is the only one of its kind in Finland, but similar pots have been found in Sweden.
Helsinki University Collections/NM Height 9 5/8 in. (240 mm.), diameter 6 3/8 in. (160 mm.)

113

Two bronze horseshoe buckles. The buckle with square ends was found in Osmanmäki, Eura, and is from c. 1000. The one with stylized animal head ends is from Myllymäki, Nousiainen, and is probably early twelfth century. Such heavy horseshoe buckles were used mainly for fastening a cloak.
NM 6127:47. 3 3/16 × 3 1/4 (79 × 81 mm.)
NM 10146:17. 1 7/16 × 1 5/16 (36 × 33 mm.)

114

Clasps and pendants from Åland. The clasp at the upper left is the top of a bronze ornamental pin formed into a pendant, and is pure Scandinavian in type. It is from the Viking period and was found in Bartsgårda, Finnström. The round clasp on the left was found in the same place, the chains and other clasp in Sundby, Sund. These are also Viking and Scandinavian in type, whereas the bronze pendant with three loops at the bottom is from the late migratory period and is eastern in origin. It was found in Mangelbo, Finnström.
NM 4780:8. 1 11/16 × 1 1/4 (42 × 32 mm.)
NM 421. 1 3/16 × 1 3/16 (29 × 29 mm.)
NM 4780:48. 1 1/4 × 1 (32 × 25 mm.)
NM 4628:91. 1 1/4 × 13/16 (32 × 20 mm.)

115

Finnish jewelry from the Viking period. The round, boss-shaped brooches were found in Laitila and Kokemäki, the flat-backed brooches in Kangasala (2) and Hattula. The nodule decoration on all these pieces is considered especially Finnish.
NM 5897:85. 3 11/16 × 1 1/4 (92 × 31 mm.)
NM 9162. 3 3/16 × 1 (79 × 25 mm.)
NM 1763:16. 2 3/8 × 2 3/8 (60 × 60 mm.)
NM 2548:267. 2 1/4 × 2 1/4 (57 × 56 mm.)
NM 6095:82. 2 7/8 × 1 1/16 (72 × 27 mm.)

116

Comb-shaped bronze pendant and three bronze boss-shaped brooches from the Viking period. The pendant was found in Kalvomäki, Kokemäki, the brooches in Eura, Kalanti, and Kangasala.
NM 1763:27. 1 5/8 × 1 7/16 (41 × 36 mm.)
NM 2031:17. 2 5/16 × 2 5/16 (73 × 73 mm.)
NM 2729:63. 2 1/2 × 2 7/16 (63 × 61 mm.)
NM 5345:1. 2 1/8 × 2 1/8 (53 × 53 mm.)

117

Bronze horseshoe buckle and bracelets from the Viking period. The pieces were found in Syllöda, Saltvik, and were imported from Scandinavia.
NM 280. Buckle 2 1/16 × 1 11/16 (51 × 42 mm.), bracelets 3/8 to 1 in. wide (10 to 25 mm.)

118

Bracelets found in pairs in Ristimäki, Kaarina, and in Mynämäki. They are probably eleventh century, the narrow ones perhaps slightly more recent than the wide ones.

NM 14349:60. Width $^3/_8$—$^{15}/_{16}$ in. (10—23 mm.)
NM 14609:1—2. Width 1 $^3/_8$ in. (35 mm.)

119
Oval Scandinavian boss-shaped brooches from Syllöda, Saltvik. Brooches in this style are from the tenth century and were the model for Finnish oval boss brooches.
NM 280. 2 $^{13}/_{16}$ × 1 $^{15}/_{16}$ (70 × 48 mm.) and 4 $^3/_8$ × 3 (110 × 75 mm.)

120
Oval boss-shaped brooches of the type used by women to fasten the shoulders of their pinafore skirts in Karelia in particular, but also in Häme, where the oldest of such brooches have been found. The brooches in the picture are from Hiitola, Kaukola, Lammi, Sakkola, Kurkijoki, Hauho, Tuulos, Noormarkku, Urjala, and Räisälä.

NM 2298:188.	NM 4636:7.	NM 9330.
NM 2520:40.	NM 4636:2.	NM 2616:7.
NM 9874.	NM 8116:1.	NM 5418:19.
NM 8116:2.	NM 2274.	NM 7276:3.
NM 1922:422.		

121
Oval boss-shaped brooches from Noormarkku and Hiitola. The brooch on the left is decorated with an acanthus motif; the other is a »crayfish brooch,» the most common type of all oval boss-shaped brooches.
NM 2274. 3 $^{13}/_{16}$ × 2 $^3/_{16}$ (95 × 55 mm.)
NM 5418:19. 3 $^3/_{16}$ × 1 $^{15}/_{16}$ (79 × 48 mm.)

122
A twelfth-century Karelian woman's costume, designed by Riitta Heinonen on the basis of grave finds in Kaukola. The skirt, blouse, apron, and veil are wool, and color analysis has been used to make the colors of the material as authentic as possible. The apron is decorated with bronze spirals. The bodice is edged with braid and fastened at the shoulders with oval bronze boss brooches, which also support the chain arrangement. The chains are connected to the brooches by »ear sockets.» Two iron chains lie across the breast, and the chains carrying the pendants are bronze. The picture shows a double-headed horse pendant, but the chains often also carried a knife with decorated haft and sheath and an ear spoon. The blouse is fastened with a round silver clasp, and around the woman's neck is a ribbon decorated with silver mountings. Finnish National Museum.

123
Bronze horseshoe buckle with lion's head ends from Varpimäki, Kerttula, in Raisio. The buckle was imported from Scandinavia and is Viking in period.
NM 11656:1. 2 $^{15}/_{16}$ × 2 $^1/_2$ (73 × 63 mm.)

124
Silver »thistle» brooch found in Untamala, Laitila. It dates from the tenth century and was imported, probably from Britain or Norway.
NM 11243. Length 14 $^{13}/_{16}$ in. (370 mm.), diameter 4—5 in. (100—125 mm.)

125
Silver necklets from the Lämsä treasure trove in Kuusamo. The necklets are thought to have been made in Karelia, which was at the peak of its cultural flowering at the time the treasure was probably hidden, i.e., 1050—1150.
NM 13350: 2,3,4,5. Diameters 6 $^3/_8$ × 6 $^7/_{16}$ (159 × 161 mm.), 7 $^1/_{16}$ × 6 $^3/_8$ (176 × 160 mm.), 5 $^{13}/_{16}$ × 5 $^{15}/_{16}$ (145 × 148 mm.), and 5 $^3/_{16}$ × 4 $^1/_2$ (129 × 112 mm.)

126
Bronze strap mounting found in Paarskylä, Perniö. It is the only one of its kind in Finland and was imported from Hungary in the later migratory period.
NM 4078:40. 3 $^3/_8$ × $^{15}/_{16}$ (85 × 24 mm.)

127
Bronze knife haft from Urjala.
NM 13219:5. Length 4 $^3/_8$ in. (109 mm.)

128
Sword pommel in a crouching-animal design from Kirmukarmu, Vesilahti. The pommel has been dated at around A.D. 600.
NM 3005:6. 2 $^3/_8$ × 1 $^1/_{16}$ × $^5/_8$ (60 × 27 × 16 mm.)

129
Part of a silver reliquary plated in gold, which was apparently worn as a pendant. The piece was found in Loposenmäki, Lapinlahti, Sakkola, and was probably imported from western Europe during the Crusades.
NM 4421:6. Diameter 1 $^3/_8$ in. (34 mm.)

130
Bird pendant found in Tuukkala, Mikkeli. Ornaments like these were hung from women's bodice chains and were common among nations related to the Finns. They appear in Finland in Karelia graves of the Crusades period.
NM 2481:78. Length 2 $^1/_8$ in. (53 mm.)

131
Bird pendant from Narva, Vesilahti, twelfth century.
NM 13939:2. Length 1 $^3/_{16}$ in. (29 mm.)

132
Decorated pine board found in the Aittoperä marsh, Pudasjärvi. The piece has not been dated exactly, but it may be late Iron Age or medieval.
NM 3487:9. 19 $^3/_{16}$ × 10 (480 × 250 mm.)

133
The bronze hem of an apron from Ristimäki, Kaarina. At the end of the pagan era, clothes were decorated with bronze spirals. Because of the bronze mold produced by the spirals, the fabric, too, has often been preserved.

Women's aprons, in particular, were probably richly ornamented.
NM 14349:99. Width 3 ³/₁₆ in. (80 mm.)

134
A bronze knife haft in the shape of a bird of prey from Hovinsaari, Räisälä. The piece is probably from the Crusades period and may be of eastern design.
NM 2298:154. Length 3 ¹⁵/₁₆ in. (69 mm.)

135
Twelfth- or thirteenth-century bird image found in Uhtua, cast in a metal compound such as bronze or brass. The bird was probably sewn into clothing and may have been made by an East Karelian caster inspired by Permian models.
NM 8767. 3 ¹/₄ × 2 ⁵/₁₆ (82 × 55 mm.)

136
Silver horseshoe buckle from Tuukkala, Mikkeli. The buckle is decorated with plant motifs characteristic of the ornamental style that flourished in Karelia during the Crusades.
NM 2481:89. 3 ⁷/₈ × 3 ³/₈ (96 × 84 mm.)

137
Woman's jewelry from Sipilänmäki, Sakkila. On the left, a knot of woven silver thread on which the veil was fixed, then filigree-decorated silver beads, a broken horseshoe buckle, and a thin silver pendant. The find dates from the twelfth century.
NM 10663:1,5,6,4,3,7,10.

138
Two silver horseshoe buckles. The buckle on the left was found in Koski, Häme, and is unique in Finland; the other is from Räisälä and has counterparts on both sides of the Baltic. The buckles were used mainly in the eleventh century, though the smaller one was perhaps not buried until the twelfth century.
NM 2306:2. 2 ¹¹/₁₆ × 3 ¹/₁₆ (67 × 77 mm.)
NM 14449. 3 ³/₈ × 3 ¹⁵/₁₆ (85 × 98 mm.)

139
Silver horseshoe buckle from Rantue, Sortavala, of a rather rare design in which the rim is convex-concave. This type was probably worn in the twelfth and thirteenth centuries.
NM 8121:2. 4 ¹/₂ × 4 ¹³/₁₆ (112 × 120 mm.)

140
Silver necklace with ax-shaped pendant from the Lämsä treasure trove, Kuusamo, which probably dates from 1050—1150. Perhaps made in Karelia.
NM 13350:1. Pendant 4 ¹/₆ × 4 ⁷/₈ (102 × 122 mm.), chain 28 ³/₁₆ in. (705 mm.)

141
Two silver brooches from the Ruuhijärvi treasure trove at Nastola, which is probably thirteenth century, and a silver bracelet from the Aatservainen treasure at Salla, early twelfth century. The brooches are of a design familiar in Karelian burial finds, though they may have been made in Gotland. The bracelet, on the other hand, is Votian.
NM 5408:2. Diameter 2 ¹¹/₁₆ in. (67 mm.)
NM 37. Diameter 2 ¹⁵/₁₆ in. (74 mm.)
NM 5408:1. Diameter 2 ⁵/₈ in. (65 mm.)

142
Silver pendants from Karelian finds in Sortavala, Rautu, Hiitola, and Sakkola. The pendants were buried at different periods, but were probably all used between the late eleventh and late thirteenth centuries.
NM 8121:5.   NM 8117:4.   NM 3641:2.
NM 8117:5,6.   NM 8121:4.   NM 10663:9,2,10,8.

143
Ear spoons from Hiitola, Sakkola, and Räisälä. Small pendants like these are fairly common in Karelian graves of the Crusades period and are thought to have been used for cleaning the ears.
NM 3247:11. 4 × ¹³/₁₆ × ¹/₁₆ (100 × 20 × 2 mm.)
NM 3247:12. 2 ⁵/₈ × ¹⁵/₁₆ × ¹/₈ (65 × 24 × 3 mm.)
NM 9415:13. 4 ¹/₁₆ × ¹¹/₁₆ × ¹/₁₆ (101 × 17 × 2 mm.)
NM 2592:9. 3 ¹/₂ × ³/₄ × ¹/₈ (87 × 19 × 3 mm.)

144 and 145
Iron swords from the Viking and Crusades periods. The sword on the right was found in Perniö and is ninth century in type; the others are from Vesilahti and Ristiina and date from 300 or 400 years later. The Perniö sword hilt has a decoration of indentations, the others are plain.
NM 6483. Length 39 ¹³/₁₆ in. (995 mm.)
NM 439:1. Length 38 ³/₁₆ in. (955 mm.)
NM 7752:1. Length 38 ¹/₄ in. (957 mm.)

146
Twelfth-century weapons decorated with silver-thread inlay. The sword was found in Pappilanmäki, Eura, and the hatchet in Humikkala, Masku.
NM 65.   NM 8656. Grave 47:5.

147
Silver necklets from the Crusades period. The chain with cross was found in Suotniemi, Käkisalmi. The chain is Scandinavian, but the cross is a copy of Byzantine models. The separate cross was found in Voipala, Sysmä, and is decorated with Karelian-style plant ornamentation and human images.
NM 2487:39. Length 29 ³/₁₆ in. (730 mm.)
NM 12400:1. 2 ¹/₈ × 2 ³/₄ (53 × 69 mm.)

148
Cross, possibly Byzantine, found in Norola, Mikkeli, made of silver alloy and probably eleventh century.
NM 10880. 2 ¹/₁₆ × 1 ⁹/₁₆ (52 × 39 mm.)

149
Tin-plated bronze cross, *c.* eleventh century, found in Ristimäki, Kaarina, of a type met with in Scandinavia, the eastern Baltic, and Russia.
NM 14349:77. 2 $^1/_8$ × 1 $^3/_4$ (53 × 43 mm.)

150
Silver cross from Taskula, Maaria, made in Scandinavia in the eleventh century. The figure depicts the Virgin Mary dressed in a knee-length skirt and wearing a cross. On the other side is a Crucifixion scene. The cross was worn on a chain of woven silver thread ending with the animal heads shown in the photograph.
NM 11275:29. 2 $^1/_4$ × 1 $^{13}/_{16}$ (56 × 45 mm.)

151
Silver niello-decorated reliquary cross from the Joensuu treasure trove, Halikko, thought to be the cache of a church thief. The central figure on the cross may be a misconceived Virgin Mary, and the human figures around her are saints. The piece is probably from Gotland and dates from the twelfth century.
NM 2570:2. 4 × 2 $^3/_8$ (100 × 60 mm.)

152
Silver niello-decorated reliquary cross from the Halikko treasure trove, probably from Gotland, dating *c.* 1100.
NM 2570:3. 3 $^1/_2$ × 2 $^1/_4$ (87 × 57 mm.)

153
The other side of the cross in plate 52, the arms decorated with praying figures, the sun, and an animal.
NM 2570:3. 3 $^1/_2$ × 2 $^1/_4$ (87 × 57 mm.)

154 and 155
The »Hansa dish» from Rantola, Kuhmoinen, decorated with the figure of an angel. Bronze dishes of this type have been found all over Scandinavia and date from 1050—1140.
NM 1232:1. Diameter 10 $^1/_{16}$ in. (251 mm.)

156
Decorated silver beads from the Halikko treasure trove, probably hidden in the twelfth century.
NM 2570:4. Largest diameter 1 $^5/_8$ in. (40 mm.), smallest 9 $^1/_{16}$ in. (14 mm.)

157
Gilded silver crucifix and chain from the Halikko treasure. The piece was made in Gotland in the early twelfth century (see plate 158).
NM 2570:1.

158
Englargement of the gold-plated silver crucifix from the Halikko treasure (plate 157). The figure on Christ's left is the Virgin Mary; the one on the right, John. The figures at the ends of the arms are angels, and above are veiled human faces thought to represent the sun and moon. The cross is believed to be from Gotland and has been assigned to the early twelfth century.
NM 2570:1. 4 × 3 $^1/_{16}$ (100 × 76 mm.)

159
The reliquary forming part of the Halikko crucifix chain arrangement. The front depicts a lion in relief.
NM 2570:1. Diameter 1 $^3/_8$ in. (35 mm.)

Typography and binding designed by Ahto Numminen

Set in Monotype Ronaldson

Printed in rotogravure, offset, and letterpress by the

Otava Publishing Co., Helsinki 1961

Paper produced by G. A. Serlachius Oy, Kangas